December 2003

For Carole,

Here's to the past . . . .
and the good times still
to come!

Regards,

Sam and Lin

POSTCARDS

FROM THE

PAST

Portraits of People and Places

POSTCARDS

FROM THE

PAST

Portraits of People and Places

SAM OGLESBY

DEDICATION

This book is dedicated to Ari and my parents.
You were always there for me.

"There's so much more embracing
Still to be done,
But time is racing . . ."

CONTENTS

PREFACE

The story behind this book is a tale of sloth and failure and my rather belated attempts to make up for those sins of the past. The failure lies in my inability, despite the best of intentions, to keep a journal documenting interesting moments in my life. More than just moments, there were events and times, peopled by unforgettable characters – family members, friends, total strangers – which needed to be remembered and shared. As a great fan of the diarists – I remember reading *Samuel Pepys' Diary* at an early age – I decided to keep my own journal documenting things that seemed important to me, but somehow it never happened, aside from a few random pages scribbled here and there over the years. Going through a trunk full of old photos and other miscellaneous memorabilia, I would come across the odd scrap of paper with some paragraphs written about a place or a person, a blank page ripped out of a paperback book on which I feverishly described how it felt being under fire in a bunker in a remote place in Vietnam in 1966, or an amateurish poem I had written, pouring out my emotions about a love that had gone sour. As much as I treasured the memories these bits of paper brought back to me, they were like specks of dust floating in the attic of my mind. They didn't tell the story I wanted to hear, the story of my life. I needed to pick up that strand before it disappeared. It would be glib and pompous to say that I was too busy living life to write about it, but we will delude ourselves with all sorts of excuses rather than admit the truth, which was that I was plain lazy.

Laziness can always be corrected with a well-placed kick, but memory, once it starts to go, cannot be summoned back that easily. I realized that my memory was preparing to exit, stage left, when a friend regaled me with a very amusing story and finished the tale by saying "Don't you remember what fun we used to have?" It didn't dawn on me even after she had finished the story that I was the protagonist. I drew a blank. I had simply forgotten the whole affair, something that should have been remembered and savored, not suppressed or forgotten. Strange to say, retirement jolted me to my senses; funny how unlimited leisure can jump-start you into action. One day, as I sat in my garden staring out into space, randomly reminiscing about everything and nothing – I can't help but think of Marlon Brando's final scene in *The Godfather* before he checks out – I knew that I had to write down those things, good and bad, funny and sad, which had made my life what it was. Why this compulsion? What was so important about MY life? It had not been especially exemplary, so what was there to say? I could not pretend to have been a role model of any sort; many people had been better and badder than I had been and had written to tell about it. Call it therapy or the whim of an old man trying to fill his time; I just had to do it.

When I turned sixty, I found myself fascinated by the fact that I had already lived most of my life. Maybe by looking back at those six decades, I would learn things

I had missed when I was too young to see the forest because of the trees. And there were issues, deeply personal feelings, that had been stashed away but not forgotten, which needed to see the light of day. The first of these was my parents. We parted company when I was a teenager. Though we lived under the same roof, I remember feeling estranged from them for reasons I couldn't even articulate to myself. Just another adolescent angry at the world and taking it out on his parents? Whatever the reasons, I moved on and "matured," but I never really came to terms with them before their deaths. How I wanted to speak to them to express my appreciation for having brought me into the world, for having raised me to the best of their abilities, for having given me some of the gifts and talents they possessed. But it was too late. It never happened because of their early deaths and my blind pride. I brooded about this sad state until a friend suggested I could find peace of mind by writing to them. I did this in the first two chapters of this memoir. "Tin Box Memories" and "Last Call" take me back to my childhood and the seeds of my bitterness towards my mother and father. My friend was right. Somehow, after writing these two pieces, a great weight seemed to lift itself from my shoulders and I found a peace of mind that I had not expected would ever come to me.

My adulthood and working life were spent mostly outside of my native land, the United States. Living abroad was fascinating, exciting, exotic; I could go on with an endless series of adjectives that would describe adventures I wouldn't trade for the world. But I also wonder what it would have been like to have spent my whole life in one place, a small place, say a farming town in Iowa or a fishing village in Maine. As colorful as my life abroad may have been, I wondered what it all added up to. Where was the continuity? The next four chapters of this book explore this question. They also delve into the darker realm of loneliness and what it feels like living on the periphery of societies you so desperately want to join, but in which you will always remain a stranger. As a foreigner living in the third world, I became acutely aware of this imbalance. In "Terres Rouges," I return to Vietnam and the futility of the War and what it did to all of us, the Americans, the Vietnamese and the French. In "Jaipong," I describe my love for the charm and mystery of Indonesia and the pain I experienced when I had to leave. "City of Angels" is a nostalgic trip back to Thailand which proved to me that, yes, you can go home again, but only for a few days. "The Golden Hour" exposes my rather complex feelings about Burma, now called Myanmar, and raises questions about what foreigners can do to "help" a developing country.

It was in Burma that my loneliness became most acute, where I ached to become part of the society, but found that it was not possible. Writing about my experience in these countries has given me new insight into life in my own country. I returned from thirty years aboard resigned to the reality that no matter how much you try, how well you learn the language, how deeply you immerse yourself in the culture, you will always be an outsider. Liked, yes, and even respected, perhaps, but always one of "them" and not one of "us." How ironic then to return to one's Motherland and feel like a stranger here too! By the time I returned to the United States, the winds of change had blown in many directions, in my opinion, not all of them good. Something called "multiculturalism," which had started in a benign and well-meaning enough way, seemed to be spinning out of control, with ethnic groups and races glaring at each other, defensively misconstruing intentions and failing to communicate at the most basic level. The "melting pot" of old may not have been the perfect answer, but what had replaced it seemed in danger of becoming a bitter Tower of Babel. I was crushed and depressed by the gloomy social atmosphere I found in my own backyard, the low ebb to which human relations seemed to have sunk. So much for togetherness. I thought of that line from Sondheim's "Send in the Clowns." "Losing my timing this late in my career . . ." seemed to perfectly describe the futility of my "coming home" when I did.

With one or two exceptions, the remaining tales in this collection are not heavy; some are even funny. After all, even in the darkest of stories, there should be something to laugh at.

Sam Oglesby
New York City
May 2003

CHAPTER ONE
TIN BOX MEMORIES

My Parents Wanted the Best for Us,
But Somehow Never Got It Right

There were four of us, my parents, my sister and me. We lived in a Quonset hut overlooking the East China Sea. Hot in summer and cold in winter, our semicircular tin box could have been off the set of *Bridge on the River Kwai*, more hospitable to rats and mosquitoes than it was to the unhappy humans who found themselves living there. When we walked on the sagging plywood floor, the building trembled and overnight weeds seemed to sprout up through the planks in my bedroom. After the sun went down and sometimes into the night, the Quonsets would "speak," emitting strange creaking sounds as their metal skins contracted after a respite from the noonday heat. Living there, I felt like a prisoner. My parents, the jailers.

Though they would never have admitted it, my parents were eccentrics. Oblivious to creature comforts, tidiness, or any sense of cozy interior aesthetic, their living habits reduced our sad structure of a home to constant disarray in spite of the efforts of a full-time maid to clean and pick up after them. Added to this domestic drabness was our house worker, Higa. Stick-thin and of an indeterminate age somewhere between thirty and sixty, her only qualification for the job was extreme homeliness, a trait my mother insisted upon when she hired domestics, ever vigilant to keep my flirtatious father out of mischief. My parents' announced goal in life was to provide for their offspring what they had been deprived of as children of the Great Depression. My mother was particularly obsessed about having enough food to eat and was always muttering a Scarlett O'Hara-like mantra to us: "You'll never have to go hungry like I did." She focused with fierce attentiveness on my sister, practically force-feeding her at mealtime. By the age of four, the child was obese.

Education meant everything to my parents, who, by their own tenacity, had fought their way out of Great Depression poverty and won degrees at prestigious universities. My mother liked to tell me how, as a full-time day student at Tulane University in the 1920s, she had held down a full-time night job delivering telegrams on a bicycle. They promised me a fully paid education at the university of my choice and bribed me to excel in school. I was given a dollar for every "A" on my report card. Education had been their vehicle to respectability, but it was also the cause of my mother's professional downfall. As a primary schoolteacher, she had been trained at a time when corporal punishment was standard procedure. More out of habit than conviction, she continued to wield the ruler long after others had abandoned it and on the eve of her retirement after thirty years in the classroom, she was fired instead of feted.

My father was an atheist and, with little difficulty, had convinced my mother to follow him. She left the Catholic Church shortly before their marriage. When I was nine or ten, she renounced her newfound atheism and suddenly decided that we all needed religion. Each Sunday morning, the household – my father excluded – would go to church. As a lapsed Catholic, my mother seemed destined to roam in a kind of theological wilderness. Every month or so, she would sample a different religious denomination and in the space of a couple of years, we were indoctrinated and baptized in a series of faiths ranging from Christian Science to basic Baptist. The only lesson I retained from these myriad teachings was that dancing was sinful. I think it was the Baptists who taught that. On a less elevated level, I learned how to masturbate at the Methodist Bible Study camp to which I was forcibly sent, kicking and resisting to the last minute until the bus doors slammed shut. These religious outings were the most dreaded part of the week for me. We always seemed to be running late and my mother, who cursed like a sailor, would dive into a stream of expletives when her corset zipper got stuck or when I dawdled. "Prance, goddammit!" She would hit me on the head with her long, black, patent leather purse to herd me into our aging Chevrolet while I whined with childlike logic, "Mother, we're going to church and you're cursing!" Watching in the background, my father seemed to get perverse enjoyment from these histrionics, reinforcing his belief that religion was a sham.

In their youth, my parents had been remarkably good-looking people. My father was a Kevin Costner look-alike and Mother had the swarthy Creole beauty that her native New Orleans was famous for. I suspect it must have been sheer physical attraction, which brought them together. There was no other reason; they were so utterly different. My mother actually confirmed my hunch in one of her wandering monologues about the good old days. It was a case of being thunderstruck across the crowded room, she said. On the eve of their wedding, she dumped her fiancée, a somewhat older, well-established doctor, for this handsome stranger whom she had met by chance at a party during Mardi Gras. How could she know then that she would live to regret it? That a few years later, romance would sour and her impulsive act would literally scar her? Mother suffered the curse of being a great beauty whose looks suddenly vanished in early middle age, leaving her disoriented about who she was. By forty-five, she had gone "Mediterranean." In the space of a few months, she became shapeless and sprouted a mustache. As she stood before the bathroom mirror shaving the black hairs off her upper lip, she seemed dazed by her physical transformation and how to deal with it. The sudden blossoming of her religious interests occurred about this time and she and my father began to sleep in separate bedrooms.

My father kept mostly to himself. He only had three or four neckties, at least one of which was heavily stained. Weekday mornings, he was the first to leave the house. Sometimes I would stand at the window and watch him walk up the street to the neighbor's car waiting to take him to work, pausing every few steps when he would get a shooting angina pain. He would stop, pluck a piece of nitroglycerin out of his shirt pocket, put it under his tongue, light up a Camel and continue walking. He came back late, sometimes smelling heavily of sake. At home, my father spent most of the time in his room, enveloped in a cloud of smoke from pipes, cigars or cigarettes. He was a voracious reader, marking pages of the books he read – mostly accounts of the Civil War and medical textbooks – with broken-off bits of matches. Sober or under the influence, my father was a very funny person. He had nicknames for almost everybody. He called my school principal "Old Castanets" because the poor man had loose-fitting dentures, which clacked when he spoke. One of our neighbors, Sybil King, was a faded-elegant Blanche Dubois-type Southern lady with a strong penchant for bourbon, known to everybody as "Sibbie." My father renamed her "Sippie." His name for me was apt, if a bit unkind. I had developed into a rather effeminate boy and he started calling me "Margaret Rose," after King George's younger daughter. Precociously mordant, I was amused by my put-down nickname. Later, in a "nobody's gonna kick sand in my face" turn-around, I morphed into a barbell-pumping gym thug with the biggest biceps in high school.

During the monsoon, sounds of rain were magnified tenfold when the nightly downpour pounded on our metal roof. And a good thing it was for muffling the shrieks and recriminations hurled by my parents at each other most evenings. Educated and intelligent people, they turned, Jekyll-Hyde-like, into raging maniacs when he descended into alcohol and my mother retreated behind a wall of jealousy and recrimination, lashing out at him about infidelities past and present, real and imagined. Arguments increasingly turned to physical violence as the evenings wore on. No way to escape, I would retreat to my room, try to do homework or just stare out the window as I covered my ears to screams, crashing glass and the yelp of our spaniel who happened to get in the way of a flying object. Not a good way for an eleven-year-old to spend his evenings.

Usually the altercations would end with my father passing out and my mother sobbing herself into silence. One night, however, the intensity of their battle increased and I emerged from my room to see my father beating my mother, his fists slamming into her breasts. To this day, I can still hear the dull thud of his hands on her flesh and her sudden wild reaction, grabbing an oscillating electric fan, jerking it out of the wall while it was still in motion and hurling it into my father's face, the blades nicking his nose and landing on his left eye.

Frantic with fear and grief, I ran across the street through the rain and banged on the door of the house facing us. My knock was answered by the neighbor, a handsome pilot whom I had seen leave for work each morning. It must have been eleven o'clock at night. Looking surprised at the intrusion, he stood, waiting for me to speak. Beyond his kind, friendly face, I could see his wife and their baby, who was asleep on the sofa next to her. Full of shame, I stood speechless and dripping wet, not knowing what to say. Before he could speak, I turned quickly and ran back through the rain to our tin box. After that night, whenever I saw the pilot, I would avoid his glance and never acknowledge his greeting, knowing he must think I was such a stupid boy to run through the rain at night and knock on his door for nothing.

Soon after that evening, I developed a sleeping disorder. I would wake up in the middle of the night crying out, "Everything's moving so fast!" My parents decided I was a troubled child and that I should be sent to a psychiatrist, but even at age eleven, I realized that I wasn't the only one who needed treatment. Years later, after my father had died and we had all grown a bit more mellow, I asked my mother why she and my father had never divorced. Her answer was classic. She said they talked about it many times, but had decided to stay together for the sake of the children.

CHAPTER TWO
LAST CALL

What Do You Say to Your Mother When You Know It's the Last Time You Will Ever Speak to Her?

I never realized my mother was ill until her letter surfaced from the avalanche of mail that hit my desk when the weekly diplomatic pouch arrived. I didn't have to open the envelope to know that something was wrong. The firm, old-fashioned schoolmarm's handwriting was gone; her steady, graceful script had been replaced by a shaky, barely legible scrawl which mounted and descended the face of the envelope like a scattering of chicken tracks. The way she wrote told me more than the words did. She said she had been hospitalized for some tests, but that she was fine and just wanted to let me know. She had never been sick in her life so my immediate reaction was to believe what she had written. Medical problems of any sort – even the usual ones – were just not part of her persona. She had gone through menopause without blinking an eye and at seventy-three didn't really need reading glasses even though she usually wore them as part of her schoolteacher's image. I put the letter away – the contents were brief and to the point – but I was haunted by that handwriting. To me, her firm, legible handwriting had always been one of the signs of strength, which characterized my mother – a statuesque, physically powerful woman who had been a champion college athlete and towered over my father by several inches. I was always in awe of my mother's physical prowess and her forceful personality. She never waited for taxi drivers and baggage handlers to deal with luggage, lifting and tossing heavy suitcases herself. Whenever we traveled by car on weekend excursions, it was Mother who drove while my father rode as a passenger, happily engaged in his own kind of origami, folding handkerchiefs into little sausage-like mice, which he would cause to jump about with a flick of his finger.

In my childhood, she played a double parent role, being both mother and father to me. My father was there, but not there – remote and brilliant, always in his study, reading and writing, surrounded by clouds of smoke. He loved anything that burned – pipes, cigarettes or cigars, especially those wavy little cigars called Crooks with their sickly-sweet smell and taste. It was my mother who did "dad things" with me. When I was seven, she taught me how to swim by lifting me onto a coffee table and moving my arms, legs and head in a simulated Australian crawl. When I was eleven, Mother suddenly decided it was time for me to drive. Oblivious to the legal driving age of sixteen, we roared off to an abandoned airstrip in her 1949 Chevy stick shift, where she browbeat me into the intricacies of the clutch and her own very demonstrative system of hand and arm signals. Later, when I was faced with the horrible necessity of navigating through a junior high school prom, Mother provided the necessary social skills in the form of foxtrot and Charleston lessons. I must have been the only teenager in the 1950s who performed those outmoded steps when everybody else was into jitterbug.

Inseparable soul mates and pals, my mother and I suddenly grew apart in the summer of my fifteenth year. Overnight, I went from being an only son mama's boy to an alienated teenager full of resentment for what I now viewed as a smothered, over-protected childhood filled with an over-sharing of confidences I didn't want to know about. As she grew apart from my father and his philandering became more open, I was the unwilling confidante; the witness who watched her sob and shake a lipstick-stained shirt in my face. There was also a hard-to-explain discomfort whenever she was around. Sometimes I felt creepy when I remembered how she had held me too close during those dance lessons, pressing me tightly to her and telling me how much she loved me. She and I suddenly became strangers. We no longer confided and joked with each other. I cold-shouldered every attempt she made at friendship and intimacy. I said cruel things to her like, "Parents are given, not chosen, and I don't know why I ended up with you." Always upbeat, never still and constantly talking the way women from the Deep South do, she became quiet and acted as if she were afraid of me. She replaced talking directly with speaking to me through a third person, or even the dog if nobody was there. "I wonder if Sammy is hungry or if he wants to go to a movie after he finishes his homework." Of course, I never reacted to these overtures, staring at her in stony silence.

As my parents drifted into their own separate spheres, establishing themselves in different bedrooms, my mother's attempts to reach out to me became ever more desperate. One day, she asked me – directly, "What have I done wrong? My whole life is my children. The only reason I go to work every morning is to provide for you." I never answered her. Before I left for college, the only time I think I spoke to her again was to tell her I didn't want her to attend my high school graduation. She cried for days. At the ceremony, there was an empty chair next to my father. When I left for college that fall, I stood stiff and turned my face when she tried to kiss me goodbye.

Over the next twenty-five years, I wandered the world. My grandmother called me the "Globetrotter." First there was the Army, which scooped me up in the draft and sent me to what now sounds like a surreal place, the Kingdom of Libya. In 1962, I had stumbled out of college after a desultory academic career where I managed to get an undistinguished bachelor's degree in six years, not without the help of lots of summer school. Mother never questioned my lackluster performance. She wrote regularly and the checks kept coming. I seldom replied to her letters; when I did, the bottom of the page was always empty, except for my name. "Love" or "miss you" were never there, but I always cashed the checks. Once, lurching home after an all-night pub crawl, I remembered a story my mother told me of her own college days at Tulane University in the 1920s. She had gone to school full time while holding down a day job, and then at night, she had a second job as a bicycle messenger, delivering telegrams. And here I was, drinking till dawn and about to cut another class.

My father died in 1966 at the age of fifty-five. He had just retired and chose to remain in Japan, where my parents had worked since the end of the Second World War. Too many Camels and gin gimlets. He used to joke about his bad habits as he sat sipping and puffing, reaching for a grain of nitroglycerine from his shirt pocket whenever the angina pains were too great. I had flown from Saigon to his funeral on Okinawa in the freezing, unpressurized belly of an Air Force Globemaster cargo plane, which was returning empty to the United States. Alone in a huge space just emptied of tanks and other weapons of destruction bound for Vietnam, I was too cold and numb to feel sadness. I thought of the nightmares, which had plagued my early childhood, leaving me cold and screaming. I would rush to my mother's arms to find warmth and quiet, somehow ashamed that I had to go to her for relief. When I saw her at the funeral, I was shocked at her appearance. For the first time, she looked old to me. Her hair was dyed a harsh dark brown and she seemed disoriented; the energy that always exploded around her was gone. We scarcely spoke and I can't remember what was said in the murmur of graveside funeral talk.

The next time I saw Mother was in Washington, D.C. She had come back to the States from Japan and wanted to get together. I had cleaned up my act and finished graduate school and was on home leave from my job with the United Nations in Southeast Asia. We went to a flashy French restaurant with waiters on roller skates. The meeting was awkward and mostly silent. I couldn't bring myself to apologize or express any of the sentiments I felt – regret, gratitude, respect, love. We said our goodbyes at the restaurant door. As it turned out, I never saw her again.

Years later, I accepted what was considered to be a hardship assignment and was posted to the United Nations office in Rangoon, Burma. Its exotic remoteness, the poverty, the weird government and the utter strangeness and isolation of being a foreigner in a hermit country where nothing – not even telephones – worked, took its toll on me. I had never been so thin, weighing scarcely 140 pounds in my six-foot frame, and in spite of a recent case of hepatitis, I drank heavily. Job satisfaction was zero and work had become a source of increasing frustration. Beneath the Asian veneer of politeness, I sensed our local staff were becoming increasingly hostile. There was talk of a strike and ethnic tension – always near the surface in a hierarchical, racially conscious society – complicated even the most mundane task in our office. As the foreign "boss," it usually fell to me to sort things out. But I had no inclination or talent for conflict resolution, being by nature the ultimate equivocator.

March 13 started out as the day from hell. I arrived

at the office with a hideous hangover. When I sat at my desk, the room suddenly began to shake and rattle violently. One of the worst earthquakes in Burma's history had just occurred. When the shaking subsided, my office suddenly filled with dozens of frightened staff members, shoving, shouting, all talking at once at me, asking if they could go home to check their houses and families. In the midst of this chaos, my phone rang. The extra static indicated it was a long distance call. Through the noise in my office and crackle on the phone, I could barely hear an American voice, saying, "This is the San Francisco General Hospital and I am Doctor Allen. Your mother, Thais Oglesby, is fading fast and wants to speak to you before she dies." For what seemed like a long time, there was silence, then the sound of gasps and labored breathing. Then I heard my mother say, "Hi, honey, I called to tell you I love you and say goodbye." By now, the noise in my office had subsided and twenty pairs of eyes watched as I struggled to speak to my mother. I told her how I loved and respected her and that anything good I had accomplished in life, I owed to her. As I spoke, I heard her breathing grow more gentle and regular, then she said goodbye. After a pause, I heard the doctor say, "Mrs. Oglesby has just left us." Realizing too late my need for privacy, the office begin to empty as I placed the telephone receiver back on its cradle.

CHAPTER THREE
TERRES ROUGES

Memories of War and Vietnam

Route 13 takes you north from Saigon to the rich, red earth of the rubber plantations. Built by French colonialists in the early twentieth century and now a rutted ribbon of road going nowhere, it still remained forbidden and mysterious to us half a century later, for though we traveled that route more times than we could count, we never touched the ground as our helicopters skimmed the canopy of rubber trees bordering the highway. Idealistic civilians fresh out of the Peace Corps and grad school, we had joined the State Department's Agency for International Development and had come to Vietnam as part of a massive effort by the United States to save Southeast Asia from Communism. We were the Quiet Americans. Our speech was peppered with the words "help" and "save" when we talked about the Vietnamese. Our goals were noble, if a bit nebulous, so we started with the basics – delivering supplies to refugees displaced by the damage of war, motivating villagers in a tentative effort at community development, lobbying for land reform. Young and fearless – some would have said careless – we would just as soon have traveled by road, jumping into a truck and delivering the loads of cement, rice and tin roofing directly to the villagers, showing them we cared and making sure the goods got to the right people. But the military brass at headquarters in Saigon would have none of it. Intelligence said the roads were insecure, even though there had never been any incidents of snipers or land mines, so we always flew. Sometimes, our choppers hovered so low that after the morning fog had burned off, we could see peoples' faces – peasants grimacing under the weight of bamboo poles, balancing baskets of ducks and chickens, hawkers sitting by the roadside selling pots and pans, school girls in their flowing, white tunics and conical hats, daring to look skyward, smile and wave at us. Plowing through the swarm of humans squatting on the highway were ancient Renault trucks lumbering their way to and from the city, loaded with bales of pungent, smoky-smelling rubber and all manner of contraband being smuggled for the business of war. Afternoons, the road was quiet, glistening in the wetness of a monsoon rain. The time was 1966 and Vietnam had been at war with itself for a generation. The French had made their exit and now it was the Americans' turn to prolong a conflict between brothers where no foreign presence was needed.

In its heyday, Route 13 was part of a grand network

of roads linking the French colonial empire in Indochina. Over the years, bombs, landmines, weather and sheer neglect had taken their toll, and now it ended as a pockmarked path disappearing into the malaria-infested Cambodian jungle. Before it petered out, Route 13 passed through a Baghdad Café frontier settlement called An Loc. Built by Ngo Dinh Diem in the 1950s as a provincial seat of government, but now in advanced disarray bordering on ghost-townish neglect, the remnants of a pretentious town plan could still be seen in grandiose mini-boulevards, roundabouts, and a small park now covered with weeds and frequented by grazing goats. A bit removed from this failed municipal grandeur was the real town, where a few thousand souls lived in tight proximity, squeezed choc-a-block into a motley assortment of crumbling, tiled, colonial-style shop-houses and more recent tin-roofed structures. Where the town ended, a red laterite road climbed slightly, disappearing into a forest of rubber trees, wending its way along a shaded lane, cathedral-like under the majestic bending arch of latex-bearing arbors.

Beyond the rubber trees was a world apart, the Terres Rouges Rubber Plantation. Run and owned by the French, the plantation covered thousands of rolling acres of stately trees, producing the "white gold" – liquid latex – which had made a few Frenchmen very rich and enabled many more Tonkinese to survive the daily struggle which had become Vietnam. A self-sufficient bubble that seemed oblivious to the war raging around it, Terres Rouges was quiet and orderly, a colonial tableau that time had seemingly forgotten. Everything was there. Its large hospital was well-staffed with

French doctors and locals bustling about the shaded pavilions from one ward to another. Nearby, an imposing Catholic chapel was overseen by an eccentric French priest and a covey of Vietnamese nuns who subserviently tipped their conical hats whenever a European happened to pass along the road in a jeep, leaving them in a cloud of red dust. Down the road were the rubber processing plants, more museum than factory with their ancient machinery and clattering conveyor belts somehow still functioning with equipment long beyond repair. During peak production, a strong odor of rubber filled the air; not unpleasant, it had the aroma of an over-cooked, heavily spiced Virginia ham. Sometimes, when the rubber trees were in full blossom, a breeze would mix the two perfumes of rubber – flower and factory – creating a most unforgettable scent, a kind of "Eau de Terres Rouges," I called it. There were also warehouses and a commissary surrounded by orderly rows of workers' houses, well planned amongst stands of banana trees, flowering bougainvillea and frangipani growth. Out of sight behind hedges, the French planters lived in manicured splendor, their villas surrounded by lush gardens leading to a nearby "Cercle," a country club where afternoon *pastis* was sipped and gossip exchanged. Complete with golfing greens, an Olympic pool, and tennis courts, the Cercle was silently cared for by barefoot servants – "boys and *boyesses*" – in starched white uniforms stylishly embellished with shiny brass buttons. Their lack of footwear put them in the "serving" class. Other Vietnamese in the plantation hierarchy wore sandals or European shoes according to their professional status, one of the many nuances in a mass of minutiae from the colonial code book, with subtle and not-so-subtle differences in treatment designed to punish and reward the natives, the net effect being to leave no doubt who was in charge. It would be a matter of high comedy if a planter came into the club tipsy, without a shirt or otherwise sartorially out of step. Let a local slip up in the same way and he would be fired on the spot.

From the Cercle terrace, with a view of their domain stretching as far as the eye could see, the planters were a self-satisfied collection of tough operators who could congratulate themselves on keeping their business alive in the midst of a raging war. They would grumble that it was not easy to "dance" with everybody – tango with the stealthy Viet Cong and the NVA (North Vietnamese Army) who roamed the rubber groves and committed the occasional symbolic murder just to say they were there; and waltz at the same time with the idiotic Americans, whose tanks destroyed their rubber trees with Agent Orange chemicals and whose psy-war guys "won" peasant hearts and minds after destroying their villages by holding "county fairs," ridiculous, rowdy events where amidst the ruin of still-smoking huts, from their armored personnel carriers, teenaged GIs would fling balloons and candy at screaming children and sullen adults, somehow hoping that would make them forget they no longer had homes to live in. Then there were those yapping, nipping dogs, the corrupt South Vietnamese military (ARVN) and the plantation *syndicat,* the Communist-infiltrated labor union, who had to be kept happy with bribes and concessions.

Still, life was good. Up at sunrise and into the rubber groves while it was still cool, their working day ended by noon. Back to their villas, after a sumptuous repast and a siesta, they would gather at the Cercle, where they talked of France and listened to the sound of distant guns and the occasional hum of a helicopter. Weekends were livelier when the "imports" arrived, young beauties from the fleshpots of Saigon, flown up in the plantation plane to entertain the bachelors and the more discreet married men. Not a bad way to spend twenty years before retiring in comfort back in France.

Young planters started their careers in their midtwenties after college. The pay was more than generous and by the time they were forty-five, if they could avoid the traps of opium and gambling, they could amass small fortunes, buying their own farms or estates in central France or Provence. On bigger plantations, there was always the chance to advance to manager-ship or transfer to Madagascar or Africa, where other plantations opened up new opportunities. In the meantime, a villa with servants and a technical support staff who did most of the work made life a piece of cake. There were always trips to Saigon and Phnom Penh and a lengthy home leave to France every two years. It was a meal ticket and a way of life worth holding on to. They would fight for their "white gold" and hope that it would never turn to "sang blanc" – white blood. As the war intensified, some of them realized they were living on borrowed time and began looking elsewhere for jobs. Others shut out reality and lived for the moment. Everybody needed rubber, didn't they?

For all their demonstrative French camaraderie, in reality, the planters could barely tolerate each other.

Monsieur le Directeur, Andre Chambord, was aloof and aristocratic. His patrician wife, Catherine, a permanent half-smile carved on her face, was the constant butt of a host of "her shit don't stink" jokes. Muffled giggles could be heard in the Cercle backrooms when, by accident, Madame met one of the bimbo weekend imports, uttering her Jackie Kennedy-like whisper: "Always a pleasure to see you again."

The deputy director and real boss, Hawie, a brawling, barrel-chested roughneck from the docks of Marseille, scarcely spoke to anybody aside from the occasional grunt through pursed lips, which clutched the ever-present foul-smelling Gaulois. Speaking no Vietnamese, his sole means of communication with the local staff was a series of crude gestures, which usually ended in a threat – a swift hand motion delivered horizontally across his throat as in the Mafia silent death signal. His opposite and the target of Hawie's withering glances was the Engineer Maillard, a sensitive, well-spoken homosexual from Anjou. His villa became a salon on weekends. Diplomats, doctors and professors from Saigon would dine on endless courses, discussing nihilism and post-modern deconstruction against a background of Mozart floating out on the tropical night. His unacceptable lifestyle was grudgingly tolerated because of his technical brilliance and social wit.

Dupoizat was the young playboy of the group. Scion of a rich family from Dijon who manufactured bicycles, he was a tennis champion in France and everybody knew his presence at Terres Rouges was just an adventure, not serious work. Then there were the foreigners, the non-French. Walz, a portly Swiss German whose idea of fun was serving boiling hot cheese fondue on a steamy tropical night and telling loud jokes (It's April – Schmidt takes a deep breath and shouts to Schroder "Spring in the air!" Schroder replies, "Why should I?"). And Rilke, a Roger Moore look-alike from Germany via the French Foreign Legion who said the only way to have good sex is to beat your partner first.

Accepted by nobody but essential to them all was Jacques Gallois, the half-breed son of a planter and his Vietnamese housekeeper. Jacques kept the Viet Cong happy and got the American spooks drunk on his French brandy. Handsome in a confusing, Eurasian way – Western from one angle, Asian from another – half of his face had been devastated by a hideous *Phantom of the Opera* scar, the result of acid being thrown at him by a jaded paramour. Once, he had warned me to beware of the local women, especially mixed breeds like himself. They had all the worst traits of both races, he said. Charming and vengeful, a deadly combination. He considered himself lucky to have survived her jealous rage. Another friend was not so lucky, he told me. His jilted concubine fed him a delicious meal, the rice laced with tiny, sharp bits of cat whiskers, just enough to perforate an intestine, a slow and painful way to go. As he lay dying, the concubine tenderly mopped his brow, singing gently to him.

For years, the French had been engaged in a delicate balancing act whose time was running out. As long as the Americans were far away and the South Vietnamese didn't bother them, the planters could deal with the Viet Cong, who had long ago infiltrated the rubber groves and the workers' labor union. Most of the insurgents had family who worked the rubber that provided their only steady meal ticket, so why kill the goose that laid the golden egg? A devil's bargain of edgy coexistence had been in play for years. The planters looked the other way when the VC moved their platoons through the rubber and the VC let the latex flow. If the Americans were too removed and too naïve and the South Vietnamese too corrupt and too cowardly to rid the plantation of Communists, what could a Frenchman do but sleep with the enemy from time to time? A barrier of mistrust and recrimination had grown up between the French and the Americans. Hardened colonialists who had known Vietnam like the back of their hands for over a century, the French felt the Americans inept and inexperienced, using Agent Orange chemical spray to defoliate their precious stands of rubber which had taken a generation to nurture, just to have a clear line of fire for half an hour against an enemy who wasn't there. Madness! *La grande folie*, they said as they gathered at the Cercle each evening. GIs, for their part, viewed the French as losers – pretentious, sour-grapes collaborationists who couldn't win their own war and now worked with the Cong against the United States.

Overnight, everything changed, unhinging the precarious balance that had preserved a nervous, non-war kind of peace. A sharp escalation of the war in 1966 brought more players to the table, raising the stakes in An Loc. A massive movement by American troops into the area was answered by the arrival of the North Vietnamese Army, the much feared NVA, battle-tested since 1954, when it had ousted the French from Dien Bien

Phu and won the first Vietnam War. Now more ruth-
less and savvy than ever, it had traveled more than a
thousand miles south to galvanize the Viet Cong, a wa-
vering collection of farm boys more concerned with
their rice harvest than with the enemy's body count.

As time passed, the mood at Terres Rouges became
grim. The planters knew their days were numbered.
Servants would disappear, just not show up for work
anymore and with rubber tappers constantly on strike,
the latex couldn't be harvested. Rubber trees were like
cows; don't milk them and the flow stops. The white
gold dries up. Tempers grew short. Some of the planters began partying too much and the well-orchestrated
colonial social order started to crumble.

The malaise even spread to the plantation hospital,
where crisp discipline was embodied in the command-
ing person of Chief Surgeon Dr. Estelle Granger. Cool,
beautiful, intelligent and elegantly arrogant, Dr.
Granger ran her hospital with an iron hand. We had
met on several occasions; each time she bombarded
me with an earful of anti-American *bons mots*, leaving
no doubt that in her mind, Vietnam should be left alone
– with France, of course, benevolently baby-sitting in
the background. She had done her medical specializa-
tion at Oxford and spoke impeccable Queen's English,
but refused to do so, insisting on speaking French as a
matter of principle, even if an interpreter were required. Even the other planters joked about their intimidating grande dame who always had the last word.

I was therefore stunned one morning when she
burst into my office, disheveled, lips trembling with rage
and tears streaming from her bruised, swollen eyes. She

recounted between sobs how she had been patrolling the hospital wards on her nightly rounds and about midnight, had come upon a group of drunken ARVN soldiers trying to sneak into the room of a young woman who was convalescing from malaria. When she ordered them to leave, they had beaten her savagely and then dragged her off into the brush and raped her. She had gone to the soldiers' commander, who said he didn't believe her, that she was probably drunk and had fallen on her face. Besides, he said, who would want to rape a nasty Frenchwoman? Near collapse, she hoarsely implored me, "You Americans are the big shots now. Can't you do something? My hospital is becoming a bordello! Everything is collapsing and nobody is in control! I don't care about myself! It's the patients! It's Vietnam!" Her words troubled me as much as the incident itself, and what she said was true. There was a vacuum and nobody was in control.

Meanwhile, the Viet Cong and the NVA watched and waited, knowing that the ARVN's cowardice and corruption would drive the Americans to distraction. This was the last straw for the French and one day, the planters' wives went down to Saigon and never came back. I saw Madame Chambord at Brodard's Café on Tu Do Street. Near tears, she asked me, "Why do the Americans fire their cannons so loud and all night? The sound gets closer and closer and the children can't sleep anymore. It's just a matter of time before they slit a white man's throat. I know. My *boyesse* told me so before she left. She's afraid to work for us anymore. You Americans will never frighten the Viet Cong with your tanks and helicopters. It's like an elephant trying to kill a mosquito. You should learn from our mistakes, but you don't. This is a sneaky enemy who can just fade away and then come back when you're gone. You'll see. I saw French boys die. My own brother was one of them. Now, it's all happening again, and so soon. I just hope we both get out of here alive." And so the French version of *Gone with the Wind* had suddenly become history. Swept away with the exotic life of the planters were jobs and a way of life for thousands of Vietnamese.

Just as the French were about to become history, the Americans arrived en masse. They shattered the quiet of An Loc's sleepy streets with their armored personnel carriers, churning the red earth into swirls of dust. Swarms of helicopters buzzed the sky and walk-talky radios crackled. An Loc ceased being a town with any semblance of order; everything was out of control. Teachers couldn't keep their students in the classroom when there was the chance to climb up on an American tank and get a hand-out. Village girls made eye contact with rowdy GIs and it wasn't long before there were huts on the edge of the rubber trees with signs like Las Vegas, Showtime, Big Mama's and the Green Door. Almost overnight, quiet village kids turned into screaming packs, yelling "Hey GI, gimme money! You want my sister? Very beautiful!"

There were different types of Americans. Green Berets and more ordinary grunt foot soldiers, Army doctors, the CIA, and all manner of military spooks. Bringing up the rear and barely visible was our contingent of civilian do-gooders, trying to win hearts and minds with our reconstruction programs that were still in the talking stage. The intelligence spooks were everywhere and were famous for their unique, "come fly with me" interrogation techniques, which involved taking two Communist suspects for a helicopter ride. Immediately after attaining sufficient altitude, one suspect would be tossed out the door, screaming to his death below while questioning would begin with the other. It encourages the remaining one to talk, the spooks said.

The young Army doctors were the happiest group. They loved the war and were on a *MASH*-like high because its gory destruction gave them so much interesting work. Not bothered by any stuffy hospital protocol or the prospect of medical malpractice, they were in charge and could perform any type of surgery imaginable, things that only more seasoned, senior doctors would be allowed to do back in the States in a big hospital. I am still haunted by one young medico who was particularly excited when a young Montagnard girl was brought into the clinic one afternoon when I happened to be visiting. About twelve years old, she had huge, bright eyes and a beautiful, quiet face. She had been one of those innocent victims hit by "friendly" fire. A grenade had exploded, removing a chunk of her scalp. Miraculously, the damage stopped before the brain. A piece of her skull the size of a silver dollar had been blown away, leaving only the thin, transparent membrane covering her cerebrum, which could be clearly seen pulsating below. I stood there, dumbstruck, staring as though I was peering through a porthole at the churning sea. She was fully conscious and I marveled at her calmness, her eyes blinking as she looked up at the young doctor from Texas. Neither spoke the other's language but they talked to each other just the same. She was taken away on a stretcher and I never found out what happened to her since I was too afraid of the answer I would get if I asked.

It was about that time that my nightmares began. I dreamt of peasants in black pajamas being thrown, screaming, from helicopters until their bodies hit the earth with a deafening thud. And young GIs whom I had seen earlier that day laughing and joking, being brought limbless, screaming and bleeding, caked with red mud, into the field hospitals, where nothing could be done but deaden the pain until they died. And the young Montagnard girl's brain. It would appear to haunt me at the most unlikely times of day or night. I could be having sex in a brothel in Saigon or attending a meeting with military brass about the defoliation of rubber trees, and there she was. Her brain even developed a little voice that cried out for help.

There we were – the aid workers, the do-gooders who weren't sure about what good we were doing. Our goals of rural reconstruction and community development grew more nebulous as the war intensified and American priorities become more military. Increasingly, "winning" became a negative idea – how many VC were killed, how many bombing missions were flown – not how many village schools were built or how many tube wells were dug. That would come later, we were told. Once, a USAID fat cat from Washington visited the province for an hour and promised the villagers a school, not just any old school, but one with water fountains and a gym! "When will we get our school?" they asked. Later, they were told. First, we must win the war.

But in the meantime, what were we to do to? Our self-esteem began to crumble. What the hell were we doing here besides witnessing mass destruction of a people? Why were we so impotent, just sitting on our asses, collecting our fat salaries and not doing anything to stop the killing and the misery? We were watching the disintegration of two cultures – Western and Asian – and ugly examples blew up in our faces every day; deceit matched arrogance, corruption answered brutality. Worst of all, we knew if we stayed, we would become accomplices in genocide, hapless spectators with ringside seats at a killing match. And then there was the physical danger. Fear gripped all of us as we sat on the dusty porch of our billet, engaging in incessant, mindless conversation, plagued by insomnia, indulging in cocktails before lunch, sexually obsessed trips to Saigon and full meals at four in the morning.

Each of us had a different monkey on his back as the days passed, consumed by heat and red dust. That red earth became an obsession, the beauty of the earth, its primal redness in the form of mud when it rained. Brutal and exquisite, the stain of the red earth on a wounded body whose flowing maroon blood merged with the deep red smudges of earth. I was going to pieces. One day, I looked at myself in the mirror – sleep-deprived and pale-faced. The living dead, I thought. A weakling, powerless to help anybody and too cowardly even to kill. Good for nothing. On impulse, I passed my hand along the window ledge in my room, where red dust had collected. With red fingertips, I smeared the dust rouge-like on my cheeks to give myself some color and strength to do something. I had to get out or crack up. We were reduced to things like that. Madness was not far away. I had become more afraid of living than of dying.

Our team of civilians was leaderless and without purpose, managed by a series of flawed characters more interested in fulfilling their private obsessions than pursuing a common goal. Stockton was from Southern California. An aging Beach Boy dude who paced about in highly polished boots, he did mostly nothing but plan his fornication trips to Saigon. *Ong Di Saigon* was his Vietnamese nickname – "The One Who Goes to Saigon." His day really started with cocktails on the porch around 5:00 P.M. As his speech became more slurred, he would brandish a rifle presented to him by the South Vietnamese Province chief, the colonel, – working himself to a pitch of thick-tongued rhetoric, shouting about taking everybody from the porch, leading them in a formation and charging the VC "out there somewhere" and "winnin' this fuckin' war by ourselves." Later, he would stagger to his bed in an alcoholic stupor, collapsing through the mosquito net into drunken snores. Stockton disappeared one day and was replaced by Benson, a brilliant career Foreign Service officer with deadly halitosis and a touch of madness in his eyes. Fluent in many languages, including French and Vietnamese, he wrote poems in classical Vietnamese and visited brothels in the rubber groves, returning from his trysts with his shirt clinging to his body, drenched in sweat. The rumor mills in Saigon had it that he had a "history," probably just too much of a maverick and a wild card for the starchy Foreign Service. So here he was at the end of the earth, in Nowheresville An Loc. Nobody stayed long in An Loc except the Vietnamese, and Benson was soon history too, followed by Lacey, a scrappy veteran of the development set who, for some reason also unknown to us, had been sent in exile to An Loc. He soon became a high-profile fixture in the town and a target of derision among the Vietnamese as he moved about with his privately hired bodyguards – two dusky Cambodian youths who were also his lovers. Fitted out with specially tailored black uniforms and M-16 rifles, they mounted the back of his jeep as he made his rounds, steering himself through An Loc, always smoking a nasty cigar. Facially, he was a replica of Truman Capote and had the intimidating habit of coming within a couple of inches from your face when he talked to you, pressing his forefinger into your chest as he spoke in a Lyndon Johnson manner, his rimless glasses close to your nose.

A sign of the futility and confusion in the American camp was that nobody really spoke to each other in a meaningful way. Any coordination on a professional level was nonexistent. Nobody seemed to know or care what the other Americans were doing. Everybody had their bosses to report to and reports to write. Deadlines and straitjacket chains of command made us totally blinkered as to what was really going on. Our particular albatross was the Hamlet Evaluation Report, an endless, Orwellian printout that asked us, on a scale of 1-10, to rate how well we were winning the hearts and minds of peasants we had never met, whose houses the American military had destroyed. Impossible to respond to even with the most serious effort, the questions were indecipherable pabulum dreamed up by Pentagon PhD desk jockeys whose field experience consisted of flying visits to Saigon, where they donned their safari suits and sat in windowless meeting rooms before flying back to Washington. Bob Hope could have done better. At least he stayed a few days and brought some pretty girls. It dawned on me one day that nobody could think straight any longer and that any chance of winning the war had been lost. That realization came to me in strange ways. It had to do with a one-legged hermit and pizza pies.

I visited the plantation from time to time to play tennis with the planter, Gallois, at the Cercle. One afternoon, while we were still on the court after the game and no one else was within hearing distance, his conversation went from the mundane to something very different. He said he had something important to tell me which could affect both of our lives and the lives of others as well. He said we needed more time to talk and asked me to his villa the following day for lunch. When we met again, it seemed like hours before he got around to what he really wanted to say.

When he was sure the servants were gone, we went out to the garden and he unfolded to me a scheme worthy of a Ken Follett novel or a James Bond movie. It was a daring plan to block the advance of the NVA, who had begun mobilizing in the rubber stands. In his daily rounds in remote areas of the plantation, he had made the acquaintance of a one-legged forest hermit who lived in the wild, keeping to himself and noticed by no one. Gallois said he had helped the hermit, providing him scraps of food and fuel from time to time. In return, the recluse said if he ever needed a favor, he would help him in any way he could. Now Gallois was going to cash in on that favor and proposed a fantastic scheme – to plant a powerful radio transmitter in the legless trouser of the hermit. This radio could beam location coordinates to the American military, who would guide bombers and fighter aircraft to VC and NVA locations, wiping them off the map.

He had chosen me as the emissary to liaise with the American side because we were friendly and I spoke French. More importantly, he said, he thought I was really a spy and that I would know how to move this plot forward. I was flattered, but also amused and a bit disappointed in his assessment of what I was supposed to be doing in An Loc. In fact, I had nothing to do with intelligence activities. Probably because I wasn't really doing anything else with an identifiable, useful purpose, he concluded I was a spook, just hanging out, waiting for some one-legged hermit to materialize. The plan sounded not only exciting, but also practical, an unorthodox but simple way to solve a big problem – tracking the elusive enemy.

I was full of nervous energy at the prospect of what I considered a breakthrough in which I could play a role. But what was I to do? Who could I trust to take this information and use it? With so many intelligence types operating in the area, literally stepping on each other's toes, there was an embarrassment of choices for me – the CIA, the Defense Intelligence Agency, the Special Forces Green Berets, the First Division bivouacking in the plantation, and my own boss, the Capote-esque cigar-chomper. I ruled out the CIA rep, a burnt-out case who spent his days writing useless reports to his headquarters using fabricated information provided by his sources who never got beyond the corner café. The Green Berets were another non-event, roaming around at night in the jungle with their faces blackened, a bunch of junior John Waynes who knew it all and trusted nobody, least of all a Frenchman. The First Division was another non-starter; they were into big guns and armor, not dealing with one-legged hermits. My own boss was unapproachable. During the day, he was hard to find and at night, he barricaded himself in his billet with his bodyguards and was not hospitable to evening calls.

That left the Defense Intell types. They lived in a highly fortified compound where the sound of loud generators formed a kind of extra barrier to entry. Occasionally, when I met them in town, they scarcely spoke. All this lent an air of seriousness to their image and I decided they were the ones to act on our idea. I should have known better. For openers, just getting into their compound wasn't easy. Yelling over the roar of the generators, I had to stare down a police dog and convince the armed guard that I needed to go inside and talk to my fellow Americans. Once inside, I sat around being ignored while they worked a crackling field radio trying to talk to somebody in Saigon about getting a couple of helicopters to fly 500 pizzas up to the First Division troops dug in by Terres Rouges. Five hundred pizzas by helicopter? It blew my mind that we were fighting this kind of war when the VC and the NVA survived for weeks at a time on a fistful of cold rice. When I finally got their attention and revealed our plan, they dismissed me with one sentence: "You should know better than to talk to the French."

I was crushed and didn't know how to face Gallois, so I avoided him. I went to Saigon and stayed as long as I possibly could. When I finally returned to the province, I found a note from him on my desk that simply said, *C'est fichu; le type n'est plus la* – "It's all washed up, the hermit's gone." In An Loc, we knew the walls had ears and the VC were everywhere. Probably the Defense Intell houseboy was one. Maybe he heard my story and put a contract out on the hermit. Or maybe he was killed by "friendly" fire. We'll never know. I just hoped the pizzas were still hot when they got to the troops.

Our dilemma about not being able to do our real jobs of rural reconstruction and community development was temporarily solved when we found something else to do – building prefab houses. Our old living quarters had been cramped and uncomfortable, sharing space with the Green Berets in their compound. The Special Forces never seemed comfortable with us there and we were never too easy about it either, thinking that in case of a big attack, they would be the first targets and we'd be taken out with them. Anyway, we were civilians, not fighters and it would be better for our image to be located somewhere else on our own.

We found a plot of land in a quiet part of town and a budget to build and had prefabs shipped up from Saigon. With them came a Korean construction crew, a tough bunch of hard-drinking guys who did nothing but work

and keep to themselves. In a few weeks a little bit of suburban New Jersey began to rise up in An Loc and our ranch houses really stood out. If blending into the local scene was part of our strategy, these buildings didn't help us at all.

I was against the project from the start, thinking we should vacate the Green Beret compound and live off the local economy in modest accommodations, like Peace Corps volunteers. Nobody wanted to hear me. I guess I had missed the point. What the prefab project really did was give everybody something to do. Even if the Koreans did everything, it was a diversion, an activity with a goal and an end where we could see that something other than destruction had been accomplished. And it gave us something to celebrate. When the buildings were completed, a grand dinner party was held in the biggest one. At the endless banquet, the night wore on and the Koreans kept drinking, singing mournful ballads. When I asked them to sing something happy, they told me, "In Korea, there are no happy songs."

I thought of Vietnam. Their music was poignant and melancholy too. For centuries, both countries had experienced continual warfare with China, then with other colonial powers, France and Japan. Should the United States be added to that list? I wondered. I walked out of the prefab into the starry night heavy with tropical fragrance. The Koreans, now red-faced and inebriated, continued to sing, their voices rising like the moaning wind. Blended with the sad chorus of songs, I could hear the heavy thud of mortars being fired somewhere out in the plantation and the hum of distant bombers. A requiem for this tragic war, where we had ringside seats.

Earlier that day, I had heard another kind of music. In the morning, I had been asked to join a reconnaissance team to travel to a remote hamlet by helicopter. We were going to hand out land titles as part of the government's land reform and redistribution program. We had to travel over what was considered insecure, Viet Cong-infested territory, which meant that we had to fly very low, only several feet off the ground, mostly over rice paddies, putting us below the clouds and avoiding enemy ground-fire. There we were traveling at nearly 150 miles an hour over fields being plowed by farmers with their buffalo, at times passing within feet of them. They gaped at us as though we were a UFO. Inside the chopper, we were all wearing earphones, listening to Armed Forces radio. Suddenly, the station broke into a rollicking Dixieland version of "Yessir, That's My Baby." Then I heard machine gun fire. Our side gunners thought they had spotted VC in the rubber trees and let loose with a few rounds of fire. As the sharp stutter of our machines guns rattled, shaking the helicopter, the peasants kept plowing and the jazz kept playing.

It was February 1968 and I was getting short. That was GI talk for coming to the end of your assignment. I made the rounds and said my goodbyes. The province chief invited me and a few others to his headquarters for a supremely Vietnamese event. With the lunar New Year, Tet, just days away, the colonel thought it would be appropriate to have a viewing of the Quin Hwa flower, a slowly opening lotus blossom which unfolds its pink petals over the course of two hours. When we arrived that evening, the large bud was closed and upright. Slowly it opened as we sipped tea and meditated on its loveliness, mortar rounds thudding in the distance. It seemed a fitting way to leave An Loc and Terres Rouges, a place once calm, beautiful and prosperous, now a sinking ship poised for extinction.

I flew out the next day for Saigon and the States. While I was in Saigon, the Tet Offensive was unleashed by the VC and the NVA. They struck almost every installation in the country and although An Loc was not spared, it survived for the time being. It was only much later that I learned of its ultimate fate. It was 1972 and I had returned to Washington, D.C. After Vietnam, I was confused about who I was and what I wanted to do with my life. D.C. was a good place to be, kind of Southern and hospitable and green with lots of brick sidewalks. I had enrolled in grad school. One day, I went to the dentist. Waiting my turn in his office, I picked up a copy of *Life* and the magazine somehow opened to a page entitled "Shock of War – Vietnam Retreat." And there it was before my eyes, a full-page color picture of An Loc totally leveled and devastated, its houses and shops pulverized like cornmeal. Nothing left but ashes and dust and the red earth, Terres Rouges. Above the photo was a caption quoting a senior U.S. commander in Saigon, "If U.S. air power had not been there to intervene, I think An Loc would have been a disaster."

CHAPTER FOUR
JAIPONG

On weekends; when I lived in Indonesia, we used to go to the Punjak, in tea plantation country an hour west of Jakarta. Punjak means "peak" or "summit" in Bahasa Indonesia, and even though our bungalow wasn't at a very high elevation – less than a thousand feet up I'd guess – we always felt we were ascending to great heights as our taxi climbed the road winding through the crowded little villages of West Java. We usually made our getaway from the city on Saturday morning; the cook, the houseboy and me, wedged into a small hired car crammed with bottles of wine, shopping bags full of cheese, bacon and other non-*halal* European food we couldn't find in the local hill station market, a sack of good rice hand-pounded from Menado or *basmati* from Bangkok and some warmer clothes for evenings in front of the fireplace. Every time I packed for these weekend trips, it seemed exotic pulling sweaters out of a closet in tropical Jakarta, where the heat always weighed on your shoulders like a silent rider. People used to say that there were seasons in Indonesia, but I never could discern what they were. Unlike Thailand or Burma, which had clearly delineated continental climates – the monsoon from May to September, cool weather from October to March and oven-hot heat for three months until the rains came – the equatorial Indonesian climate, like the personality of its people, was steady, sultry and hot all year round.

I lived in a tiny house in Menteng, the garden district of old Jakarta where idiosyncratic little streets named after national heroes were lined with Dutch colonial houses, set back amidst lush vegetation of infinite variety. So fertile was the volcanic soil and so generous the rainfall that even newly planted fence posts would start to grow, sprouting blossoms after a few months. A riot of flame trees, bougainvillea, hibiscus, frangipani and jasmine lent color and perfume to the neighborhood; even the simplest dwellings looked beautiful in this florist-shop setting.

Time had a special quality in Indonesia that clocks could not capture, that couldn't be measured in minutes and hours. It was in other ways that you realized what time of day it was. For me it was the daily parade of street vendors, as regular as clockwork, each having his own special sound. In the early morning, there was the knife sharpener who advertised his presence by rattling what sounded like dozens of keys as he made his rounds on an ancient bicycle; then there was the "woop-woop" of the vegetable vendors hoping to catch cooks and housewives before they left to shop in the markets; an hour or so later came the man with a push-cart, selling feather dusters and brooms. His cry was "BWEEE, BWEEEE!" uttered in a rapid, sharply rising tone as though somebody had sneaked up behind and suddenly goosed him.

After lunch, when the streets were quiet in the grip of midday heat, you could hear the frail voice of the "pillow lady" calling out in what almost sounded like a death rattle, "Batik! Batik!" Even frailer than her voice, the pillow lady must have weighed no more than eighty pounds. She was one of those creatures you couldn't assign an age to; she could have been fifty or eighty. But I wouldn't have called her a crone because she was so lively and hopped about like a little cricket. Standing well under five feet and dressed in an ancient, tattered, but softly beautiful sarong, she sold pillows of all shapes and sizes, covered in the rich, earth-colored fabrics of her native Java. I knew that it was customary to bargain in all Indonesian commercial transactions, but I felt mean doing it with this tiny person who was asking the price of a pack of cigarettes for her matchless, hand-stitched treasures. "You must bargain!" my houseboy would whisper to me, "Otherwise, she won't respect you!" My negotiations were always half-hearted and the pillow lady seemed to realize my dilemma as she sat quietly on the reed mat in my living room under a slow-moving, creaky ceiling fan.

Still later, in answer to the afternoon heat as it grew more intense, there was the tinkle of bells when the

iceman came to the rescue, sawing off blocks or chips according to the need of the customer. The end of the afternoon brought sagging energy and the rattle of stones in a tin can, signaling the arrival of a masseur, often blind, who would knead you back to life. And to complete the cycle of revival, there was always the pretty *jamu* peddler, her batik sling loaded with Johnny Walker bottles full of a pastis-colored liquid, reputed to contain essence of rhinoceros horn and the tears of virgins, calling out, *"Jamu! Jamu!"* as she hawked that mysterious, energizing elixir for which Indonesia is famous.

Even if we didn't see the evening shadows lengthening on the road, I would know that nightfall was near when the food vendors' cries pierced the night air. First was the bleat of the Madurese *satay* man –"Teh! Teh!" short for *"Satay!"* For some unknown reason, all *satay* vendors in Indonesia are from Madura, the island next to Bali. Madurese are handsome in a fierce, pirate-like way with big, wild eyes and, like Sicilians, they are all reputed to carry daggers tucked somewhere in their

black, billowing trousers. Their pushcarts were like romantic ships of the night, sailing up dark, rain-
drenched streets lighted by a single kerosene lamp dan-
gling from a gaily-painted roof. I often patronized the
satay carts but seldom ate what I bought because the
satay was inedible. Grisly and tough, rumor had it that
the meat came from any creature that walked or

crawled. For
me, it was
more the
experience
of being in
the street
and enter-
ing its life,
feeling like
I had almost
become an
Indonesian,
buying from
these forbidden carts which we had been warned off
of by the American Embassy doctors and their advice
about boiling everything twice before eating it. I would
squat on a tiny wooden stool provided by the vendor,
almost touching the ground. From that vantage point,
I felt I was entering their world as barely audible broad-
casts of shadow-puppet plays would float down the road
in sing-song Javanese, mingling with the smell of clove
cigarettes, the gentle laughter of the *bejak* (pedicab)
drivers and the background chorus of cicadas buzzing.
Finally, from evening till dawn, there were gongs and
the clack of sticks against bamboo with a rhythmic,

samba-stepping beat that made you want to dance out the door to the street to see what food was being cooked – *bak so* (rubbery fish balls) in broth, a variety of *mee* (noodles) fried or in a liquid, and a selection of *soto* – soups for which Indonesia is famous. *Soto sulung*, made from tripes, was especially prized and was sought after by drunkards since it is guaranteed to prevent hangovers.

In those days, I was a great fan of *soto sulung* since much of my time was spent acquiring hangovers, getting rid of them and acquiring them again. I lived in a constant state of alcohol-induced buzz, which was not unpleasant and did not seem to impinge upon my lucidity, even though it probably did. I even liked the hangovers that had an edgy graininess, sort of like the rough scenes played in an old film noir. Although I tended towards moderation during the week, Friday night was one long happy hour, the result being painful, head-splitting silence on Saturday morning as we made our way by Blue Bird Taxi to the bungalow in Cisarua. Each honk of the horn and bump in the road magnified a thousand times my self-inflicted misery, which would probably be repeated in a few hours before lunch as I sought relief from the hair of the dog with a glass of white wine or a tequila tonic.

Somehow, a hangover seemed an appropriate mindset as we made our way through the urban concrete grit to the superhighway out of town. Honking our way through the gridlock of traffic and urchins hawking newspapers, flowers and cigarettes, we passed a huge bus terminus. Thousands of people were milling about, waiting. Waiting for what? I wondered. Peasant women in worn batik clutching snotty-nosed children, struggled under huge cloth sacks carrying all of their worldly possessions. They stood, disoriented, squinting up at the glass skyscrapers glistening in the morning sun, refugees from rural poverty who had come to the big city to find work, adding to the masses of urban poor who picked through the city's mountainous trash heaps for food or because they had nothing better to do. A woman pushing a cart full of reeking garbage passed near our taxi. Sitting on top of the fetid pile of refuse was her baby, wobbly headed and barely old enough to hold himself erect. They were both laughing; the mother talked while the baby drooled in response.

Pickpockets cut through the crowd like bloodthirsty sharks, operating in teams of three or four. I could spot them a mile away. When I rode the buses in Jakarta, I was surprised how good my reflexes were; slapping their slimy hands away from my pockets like an onslaught of vicious mosquitoes. The pickpockets had come to the wrong place. Small chance that they would find any loot in this crowd of paupers. If they made a false move and got caught, the desperate crowds of rag pickers could have turned on them with murderous ferocity, beating them to a bloody, lifeless pulp. Such was the law of the concrete jungle of Jakarta.

For a moment, our car was gridlocked in the sea of humanity. A beggar holding a child grasped her deformed hand, rapping it against our window like a bird's claw. My cook rolled down the glass and slipped a couple of coins into her dirty, outstretched fingers. Somehow we managed to get through the man-swarm without incident, avoiding those money-seeking troublemakers who would throw themselves against the car with a loud crunch and a moan, hoping to collect money from a car carrying a *buleh* (white foreigner).

We reached the turnpike tollgate and moved into the slow lane. Our taxi was an aging Toyota that couldn't keep up with the BMWs and Benzes whizzing past. The fog of my hangover cleared, jolted by the inequality of the poverty just seen compared to the carefully coiffed, designer-clad drivers of the luxury cars now leaving us behind in the dust. The boredom of the highway lulled us all into nodding slumber. As I blinked between dozes, I saw that we were starting to climb and the silhouette of volcanic peaks appeared on the skyline.

We slipped off the super-highway onto the old, two-lane road leading to Cisarua. When we got to the village, Ibu Marsini, the cook, wanted to stop to buy eggs, watercress and fresh fish. The fish is always good in Cisarua; every farm has its own fishpond. She left the car and hobbled, stiff-kneed, into the shady tents of the market which gave out pungent odors of shrimp paste, dried fish, durian and coconut oil. We waited for what seemed like an eternity, with the midday heat beating down on the metal roof of the car. After half an hour, I got worried about where she was and sent Triyono, the houseboy, to find her.

A few minutes later, they both returned, carrying the fish in a plastic bag, convulsed with laughter. I asked her what's so funny and she refused to tell me, but kept on laughing. I threatened to withhold her salary and leave her on the road if she didn't tell me and she still kept shaking with laughter. Finally, she told me. As is common in West Java, the old farmer who sold her the fish had built his outdoor toilet directly over his fishpond, providing a convenient and regular supply of food for the fish. Due to a commotion in his house that morning, he had arrived later than usual for his regular visit to the fishpond. When he finally got to the outhouse and settled into his squat over the pond, the fish were so impatient with hunger and his late arrival that they leaped up and grabbed his balls as he was relieving himself. For the rest of the day, Ibu Marsini was so seized with spasms of laughter that I thought of taking her to the hospital. Instead, I gave her a Valium, which knocked her out cold and we had no dinner that night. The impatient fish had to wait till the next day to be consumed.

Our bungalow sat on the edge of an emerald-green rice terrace, fed by babbling water that irrigated the fields. Unlike most weekend retreats that were luxurious compounds surrounded by high walls and policed by uniformed security guards, our cottage was in the village, one of six houses surrounding a freshwater swimming pool shielded by a grove of clove trees. During rice harvest, the farmers would dry their paddy along the borders of the pool, spreading the stalks out in bunches resembling beautiful fans, like patterns in a batik print. Each task performed in this rural

 s e t t i n g
seemed to
be a work of
art – the in-
tricate criss-
cross design
created by a
p l o w e d
field, the fra-
grant heaps
of cloves waiting to be collected, their jeweled shapes highlighted in the afternoon sunlight, the tea pickers' huge
wicker hats dotting the landscape as they delicately
snipped tea leaves from the rows of hedges one leaf at a
time. A natural exhibition far better than any museum or
art gallery.

Farther in the distance, rolling hills of tea plantations stretched as far as the eye could see, specked
with ochre rooftops and a silver dome of the village
mosque. Sometimes, the play of mist and clouds
would transform the landscape into a silkscreen
painting which was set to music when the haunting
strains of *jaipong* drifted over the hills, from where,
we never quite knew. *Jaipong* was the music of Sunda,
that part of Indonesia otherwise known as West Java.
Sung, played and danced, *jaipong* was at the same
time poignant, sensual, playful and melancholy. As a
dance, it was snakelike, voluptuous and seductive;
sung, it was plaintive and spoke to the soul; played
on the flute, it was like the flame of life flickering in
the wind. To me, the sound of *jaipong* was a narcotic.
Hearing it transfixed me.

I always seemed to understand what the confusion of Indonesia was all about when I heard the magic sound of *jaipong*. It became a symbol for me of all that was strange and inexplicable about this fascinating country.Indonesia – Java in particular – is a place of contradictions, where traits found in the Southeast Asian personality are carried to their most extreme – inscrutable, refined, seemingly submissive to a degree that seems to defy human nature. A joke has it that if you step on a New Yorker's foot, he will shout at you and tell you to watch where you are going. If you step on a Javanese's foot, he will apologize for being in your way. A white man quickly becomes the bull in the china shop when he comes to Indonesia, crashing into the crowded, delicate furnishings as he enters a hallway of crazy mirrors where nothing seems familiar. There is no place for confrontation and no word for refusal or "no" in the Indonesian language, making the white bull in the china shop even more assertive and aggressive than he would be in his native Europe or America, knocking down more cabinets and breaking more china, always having his way. No one stands in the bull's path, confronting him, telling him when to stop. He is the master. But there is a price to pay as he unwittingly self-destructs.

Equally baffling, there is no place for the individual, and use of the personal pronoun "I" is considered self-centered and rude. It is always "we." This tightly imposed straitjacket of social harmony is enough to drive a white man mad! Why do they say "we" when there is only one person in the room?

And yet, "amok" is an Indonesian word. Push them too far and these seemingly submissive souls suddenly become wildly murderous. Buried not so far under the tightly controlled surface, there is a wild freedom and anarchy lurking in every Indonesian heart. No middle ground with Indonesians, no kvetching or arguing. It's either smiles or daggers. A game of Russian roulette for the white man who lives in Southeast Asia, always fated to remain the bull who never learns how to negotiate in the china shop, he lives on borrowed time, zigging when he should zag. Sooner or later, disaster comes when he hangs himself with his own rope. White men seldom survive in the Asian tropics. If they do, they are half-mad drunkards who listen to *jaipong* like mice following the pied piper.

The French call this fatal seduction *le mal jaune* – yellow fever, a lethal attraction that ultimately leads to their destruction, both physical and mental. It took me a few years before I succumbed to the fever, and I can't say I wasn't warned. I remember the moment very well. I had been in Southeast Asia a few weeks – I was in Thailand then, not Indonesia. I had gone there to work in the north, in the mountains outside of Chiang Mai. It was late afternoon and we had stopped to rest on the crest of a hill; the sun was setting and there was a sweet stillness in the air. Temple bells stirred in the breeze. A hawk flew overhead in the distance. Everything seemed so perfect and I felt at peace with myself, a feeling I had never had before. I turned to the young Australian I was hiking with and said, "I love it here in Thailand. I

could live in this country forever." He looked at me
with squinty eyes and a saddish smile and laughed,
"Mate, get outta here while you can . . . before it's
too late. I've been here five years and I'm a goner.
It's too late to leave. I'm stuck in the quicksand." It
took me a few years to realize that day on the
mountaintop, I had encountered my first case of yellow fever.

A single white man living in the Asian tropics leads
a lonely life. His compatriots have no time for him:
"Decadent, not a family man, no future, that one."
His servants who, at best, only half understand him,
are his only family. And they are no family at all since
their loyalties and responsibilities are already claimed
by blood, which is thicker than money. Being lonely
in Indonesia is different from the loneliness experienced in the West. It is not that one leads a solitary
existence for there are always people about and conversation fills the air, talk being considered a virtue
and not a sign of idle vice. And it's not that there is
hostility or a lack of friendliness; everyone smiles and
a serious face is considered antisocial.

It is a deeper kind of loneliness for which there
is no remedy. It is that solitary sense of isolation that
comes when we know we are not really accepted by
the culture and people we so desperately want to be
a part of. We can learn the language, we can eat with
our hands, we can stay up till dawn watching a
shadow-puppet play, but no matter how hard we try
and how much we crave it, we can never really inte-
grate and be part of the family, the Asian family. Our
white skin and red hair and long noses prevent it

from happening. So we try to escape from the reality of rejection and the loneliness and self-hate it creates. We bury ourselves in books. We seek the solace of alcohol, we surround ourselves with music, collect antiques, have serial sexual encounters. We become eccentrics surviving in a fantasy world of *jaipong*. Life becomes a pack of lies. That is the white man's burden. The tragedy of that burden is that it is self-imposed. What is to prevent me from leaving the tropics, from going back to Maine or Long Island? Nothing. Except that I am no longer capable of leaving. I can't go back to a place I no longer know or love. This strange country, Indonesia, this country with its corruption, its cruel class distinctions, its grinding poverty, its glorious culture, its seductive, inaccessible people, had become my country. It was now my native country, but I was not its native son.

Family or not, they were all I had, this old cook and the houseboy. They took care of me, or made me think they did. And at least they were honest. Triyono was in his twenties and like many Southeast Asian men, petite, having a pronounced feminine quality without being effeminate. Handsome in a rather delicate, childlike way, he was soft-spoken in the Javanese manner, always smiling, but the gentleness of his smile was belied by a pair of shifty black eyes that worked the room, flicking back and forth as his mind watched a scenario unfold. Somehow, when I thought of Triyono, the image of treacle appeared. He was treacly.

As is often the case with newly arrived expats, I had inherited him from my predecessor at the of-

fice, a diffident Burman with a domineering wife
and a houseful of children. As Asians are wont to do
with their help, they kept Triyono working round
the clock, following the old axiom that a busy servant is a happy servant. According to Ma Win, the
Burman's chubby wife, Triyono "loved" helping her
with her sewing and fancywork, crocheting happily
into the night after he had finished a full day cleaning, doing the laundry, gardening and cooking. I at-
tribute this working environment – slave labor with
a smile – and the radical change that took place when
he came to work for me as the cause for his frequent
bouts of depression and fits of quirkiness while he
was in my employ. For, in fact, there was almost no
work to do in my house and the solitary idleness of
the long days took its toll on someone not used to
free time or being alone. He didn't seem to survive
the transition from being a happily overworked *babu*
in a busy Asian household to his dubious elevation as
a gentleman's gentleman in an eccentric bachelor's
pied-à-terre, where the most important task was mixing gin and tonics and helping facilitate my numerous assignations. Never mind the dust on the furniture and the sour smell of the laundry, which he
would soak for a week in warm water in lieu of actually washing it. I was oblivious at that stage of my life
to the niceties of civilized living.

On those rare occasions when I actually asked him
to do some real work like moving a piece of furniture or carrying a load out to the car, he would be
seized with vapors and a headache and would have
to retire to his room. On shopping errands, he was

equally hopeless. I remember one day sending him to the market to buy a chicken. He returned instead with four wineglasses, saying he thought we needed them more than the chicken. But he made the perfect gin and tonic and some of his eccentricities amused me.

Once, a friend from Paris stayed with us for several weeks. Upon leaving, she consigned an old black dress she had been wearing to the trash basket, saying it had seen better days. Three days later, I was surprised to see Triyono wearing her black dress when he served me my evening cocktail. He said nothing about why he was wearing the dress and acted as though it was a piece of clothing made to order for him. I realized it had nothing to do with homosexuality – he was straight and I later learned had a wife and two children – or cross-dressing; it was simply the eccentricity of Java, the madness of *jaipong.*

Jaipong was alive and well in our household. Late one night, I heard a knock on my bedroom door. It was Triyono. With a leer on his face, he beckoned me to come out to the verandah, which gave onto a wild, jungle-like garden overgrown with orchid vines and huge tropical plants, including several Venus's flytraps and a wall of narcotic nightshade. There on the terrace were several hundred sleek black rats contentedly drinking milk from several gigantic bowls that Triyono had laid out for them. He looked at me, still leering, and simply said, "Lots of rats!" I returned to the living room, sat down for a moment in the darkness, trying to figure what it was all about and began to work my knee into a whistle. I was recovering from an operation after falling in a drunken stupor on a dock where I had split open my knee a few weeks earlier. I had been sent to Singapore for surgery and the wound had healed in a funny way, developing a kind of air pocket under the skin. By manipulating the knee and pulling the skin back and forth in quick jerks, I could produce a whistle. So there I sat, making my knee whistle while the rats drank their milk, several hundred little pink tongues lap-lapping at the same time. *Jaipong.* In my household, we were all seized by it, the cook included.

Ibu Marsini was a grandmotherly soul with a kindly face who dressed in the traditional sarong and *kabaya* and always wore a headscarf when she went outdoors. I never knew exactly what her background was except that she had been a gem and gold merchant at one time and that she had no use for men, having been jilted several times in her youth. She was a brilliant cook and could prepare any Western dish without ever having tasted European food in her life. Her two loves were praying and gambling. Devout, she scrupulously fasted during Ramadan, even in the final days when most people had begun to cheat and sneaked food during the daylight hours or pretended they were ill to get dispensation to do so. She was always ready for a card game, playing straight through till dawn, when we went to the mountain bungalow. At her side at all times was Choo-Choo, her five-year-old grandson. In spite of my constant efforts at friendship, it was plain that Choo-Choo didn't like me and would try to hide whenever I came in the room. A rather dull-looking, frog-faced child, he would cling to her skirts, sucking his thumb and regard me with bewilderment and terror. I wanted to send him to the local kindergarten, hoping that exposure to the outside world would socialize him, but his grandmother refused, saying the other children would beat him up.

Her arrival some months after I moved to the house was a great antidote to Triyono's idle loneliness and they became fast friends. The house was filled with laughter when the two of them were in the kitchen together and although I could not understand their Javanese dialect, I gathered that Triyono would often tease her to elicit the shrieks and roars of laughter she would produce almost non-stop for hours. In time, we discovered that Ibu Marsini was *latta*, afflicted with the Tourette Syndrome. She was particularly sensitive to sudden noise. I first noticed this one day when the wind slammed the kitchen door shut with a loud bang. Ibu cried out "Tits and balls!" Triyono crept into the room and slyly opened the door, leaving it slightly ajar so that the wind would catch it again. In a few seconds, another gust of breeze hit the door. As it closed with a resounding clap, Ibu took a deep breath, rolled her eyes and shouted out, "Twats and cocks!" never realizing a few seconds afterwards what she had said.

As time passed, the rational world of Western logic grew more distant and unreal to me. Unexpectedly, my own initiation into the shadowy sphere of spirits came through a faith healer. For months, I had been wracked by pain so severe that I could scarcely walk. Doctors had diagnosed my problem as arthritis, but I found no relief from any treatments that were undertaken. The pain in my knee was unbearable and made my life miserable. As a last resort, I went to an acupuncturist, but to no avail.

One day in my office, a young secretary named Sylvie approached me and asked if we could speak. I had noticed her among our local Indonesian staff members, but had never had the opportunity to talk to her at length. She was a quiet person and seemed so meek that I had dismissed the possibility of ever getting to know her. We sat down in my office. Her personality underwent a transformation and she took control, especially unusual when a young Asian woman and an older western man of senior rank are alone together. She said she noticed that I had been limping and appeared to be in pain. She wondered if she could help me. I looked into her face and despite its youthful gentleness, felt an almost overpowering energy coming from her eyes, so strong that I had trouble sustaining her glance. I said that I would be grateful for any help I could get since I had given up hope of being cured. She said that she would pray for me and that each evening I must drink the special water she would give me, which had been blessed. She also asked for my photograph.

Over the next ten days, I drank the water from the bottle she had provided and met with her every day in my office. During our meetings, we would close our eyes and pray silently together. On the tenth night after we began our sessions, as I was lying in bed struggling to get to sleep, I suddenly felt all pain disappear from my knee. It was as though a switch had been turned off, erasing all the agony and discomfort. I looked at the clock on the nightstand and saw that it was 11:32 P.M. The next morning, I woke after a sound sleep and went to the office. My knee was completely normal. Later that day, Sylvie came to my office and asked me how I was. I said I was cured. She said she already knew that because at 11:32 the previous night, she had focused

all of her powers on my photograph, praying for my recovery. Later that week, I spoke with a doctor who had spent many years in Indonesia. I told her my story and she said that medical science cannot explain many things that happen. I like to think that it was *jaipong* that came to my rescue.

In Asia, things have a funny way of coming full circle. I remember one winter in the early 1960s, when I stopped in Tokyo on my way back to Vietnam from R and R. I was in my mid-twenties and went out on the town with my Japanese godfather, Ishikawa-san. He had been my father's closest friend when they worked together in Intelligence during the American occupation of Japan after the Second World War. Something about heavy water hydrogen and nuclear fission in North Korea, all very hush-hush.

Ishikawa-san took me to the teahouse where he and my father had caroused for years, introducing me to the mama-san and her girls as the new generation – the son of his best friend and one of her best clients. She remembered my father; the American who could sing the Japanese national anthem, drink sake nonstop and recite off-color spoonerisms.

There was a buzz and excitement in the teahouse that evening because the bar next door had just been visited by the president of Indonesia, Sukarno, another world-famous womanizer. He had taken away a girl whom he had renamed Devi. Sometime after that, I heard from Ishikawa-san that Sukarno married her and took her back to Indonesia.

Twenty years later, when I was living in Jakarta, I attended a pretentiously grand dinner party hosted by one of the expatriate oil company fat cats who had made a fortune with his Indonesian partner in the post-Sukarno kleptocracy. Seated next to me was a heavily painted enamel face, decorated with a kilo of gems and enveloped in a cloud of cigarette smoke. It was this same Devi Sukarno, the former first lady of Indonesia, now a merry widow of a certain age. I complimented her on her beauty and her jewelry and noted that she was wearing Shalimar perfume. "Sukarno's favorite," she said, dragging on her cigarette, still with the raucous voice of the Ginza demimondaine. "He always wore it himself, you know." It was good to hear that the founding father of Indonesia was also a child of *jaipong*.

Although I tried not to think about it, I realized that after five years, my time in Indonesia was coming to an end. What could I do? I desperately wanted to remain in this mesmerizing place that had taken such a grip on me. Excluding missionaries in the bush, I had already stayed "in country" twice the length of time normally expected of most expatriates. I knew that my reputation at headquarters had already suffered by my insisting on staying so long in one country. Time and again, I had refused new assignments with the promise of promotion. I found one pretext or another to convince my superiors not to take me away. How could I possibly leave my little house in Menteng, rats and all? What would I do on weekends in another place without my bungalow and its rice terraces and the haunting strains of *jaipong* to soothe me? Indonesia had claimed me for its own and I had to stay, whatever the price. I had fallen into that dreaded category labeled "gone native," which carried with it the meaning of "no longer knows what's he's doing; can't think straight; acts like a local." I had to make a choice: leave or throw my career down the drain, quit my job and remain in Indonesia, teaching English or doing whatever I could to survive. But staying would be impossible in any case, for the simple reason that I couldn't get a visa to remain in the country legally.

I became paralyzed with panic and depression. Then one night, I received a phone call. It was headquarters, with one final offer: go to the Kingdom of Bhutan. The following week, I packed my bags and said my goodbyes.

The last trip to Puncak had been sweet and sad, the air purer, the rice fields greener than ever before. I bid farewell to Ibu Marsini, who had become a mother to me. As the plane climbed high over the red roofs of Jakarta, I was surprised to find myself breathing a sigh of relief and thinking to myself as I remembered that day so long ago in Chiang Mai. "Against all the odds, I got out before it was too late!" Then I laughed to myself, knowing that *jaipong* would find me again in Bhutan, or wherever I went.

CHAPTER FIVE
BACK IN THE CITY OF ANGELS

How can I describe the essence of Thailand? That feeling that creeps into your heart and mind and bones when you live there? Some say Bangkok is canals and temples, palaces and riverboats, but most of all, it is people. People who infuse the city with an ethereal quality quite unlike any other place I've ever been. More than just people, it is a collection of characters – Buddhist souls – who see themselves marking time, living out the thousands of lives they are fated to follow until they reach nirvana and liberation, never to be born and suffer on earth again. There is a bemused detachment in the way Thais behave; like butterflies on the wall of life, they watch themselves as they play out this existence before moving on to the next cycle, never taking anything too seriously, never hating or loving too much. The middle path, they call it.

In the years I lived there, how many times would I be admonished, "Don't be so serious and don't 'think' so much!" Don't brood! Don't be intense! Have fun! Thais seldom brood; in fact, "thinking" seemed alien to their nature, a rebellious act which goes against the flow of destiny that Lord Buddha said must be followed and not resisted. Contented resignation fills the air. I felt it the day I arrived in Thailand.

It was August and the monsoon was in full swing.

Rain in Thailand is serious stuff; not your genteel April shower, but a steady downpour like endless buckets of water that lasts for five months from May till October, flooding the streets, causing things to just float away. Sidewalks become an elaborate lattice work of planks superimposed on the pavement so pedestrians don't have to walk ankle deep in water; taxis chug along with water lapping at their fenders, motors expire at an intersection, creating chaos; people get drenched. But nobody seems to mind. "It doesn't matter" is the national slogan in Buddhist Thailand.

I remember that first day back in 1973. I had come

to Thailand to work at the United Nations and was staying in a hotel a few blocks from my office while I hunted for more permanent quarters. Next to the hotel was an exotic shrine crowded with people and clouded with billowing incense smoke. From my room, I heard the tinkling sounds of a small orchestra playing in the corner of the shrine and leaning from my window, I glimpsed groups of tiny female dancers, faces powdered a ghostly white and dressed in heavy gold brocade, tilting and swaying with outstretched arms before gilded statues half-buried under orchids and offerings of fruit. The smell of incense drifted up to my window, blended with tropical flowers being offered by the worshippers to the Hindu god, Erawan.

The shrine had become famous because it was believed that a construction accident had occurred at a nearby building due to the failure of the builders to offer homage to Erawan before they started their project. Recognizing their mistake, the builders had constructed this elaborate temple to atone for their oversight. Since then, nothing had gone wrong. The Thais believe that bad things happen when the gods are neglected. Spirits hover everywhere amongst us; ignore them at your own peril.

The next morning was my first day of work and I prepared carefully for it, selecting a wardrobe that would impress my new boss and his colleagues. His name was Wali Shah Wali and he was an Afghan prince. I knew the importance of appearances, especially with people like that, so I dressed carefully. I had to come across as a serious young professional. Ready to begin my new life, I stepped out on the street in the pouring rain, holding an umbrella with one hand while I gripped a briefcase with the other. I had decided to walk to the office since it was only two blocks away and, in any case, getting a taxi would not be easy. I made my way carefully down the road, weaving through the crowds and the street vendors. It was chaos with hundreds of people moving in every direction along a narrow, flooded sidewalk, but it was a harmonious kind of chaos. Everybody seemed to move together in a friendly, collective rhythm unlike a similar crowd in New York City, which would be shouting, elbowing, bumping and cursing. I was managing pretty well, halfway there and still dry. My shoes were getting a bit damp, but that didn't detract from my overall appearance – well-tailored, medium-tan safari suit, brown shoes from Brooks Brothers, serious briefcase. At thirty-three, I cut a nice figure, nearly six feet tall, short haircut, not too heavy and not too thin, a dedicated look on my face almost like that of a missionary's. The kind of persona that could fit in. I hoped the office would be pleased with me, their newest expat staff member.

I could see the office building just yards away now and miraculously, the crowds in front of me on the sidewalk seemed to disappear. So much the better; I wouldn't have to tangle umbrellas with a dozen more people before getting to my destination. Umbrellas were necessary, but what a drag. I almost got the corner of one in my eye a few steps back. The Thais are so short their umbrellas end up hitting me in the face. I noticed a stall to my right where a portly Thai lady was selling fried bananas. The aroma hit my nose and I realized I had been so nervous and preoccupied with my appearance and my elaborate toilet that I hadn't even had breakfast that morning. The banana lady caught my eye and seemed to have a frown on her face. Maybe she didn't like foreigners. I heard that the Thais were friendly people, but there is always a bad apple in every crowd. Suddenly, she started yelling at me and gesturing. How could I possibly know what she was trying to say? Even if I spoke Thai – and I was planning on learning it – I couldn't actually hear what she was going on about because of the noisy downpour. I'd better ignore her or there might be trouble. Just walk on as though nobody was there. That's what I had done in the South Bronx when people tried to hassle me. Tunnel vision and fast forward; don't lock eyes with anybody. I took a few more steps and suddenly, in less than a second, I had disappeared. I found myself neck-deep in water, having fallen, feet down, through an open manhole into a sewer.

Still submerged, I kept holding the umbrella and my attaché case, containing what were now totally soaked briefing papers and other documents, including my passport. I must have looked like the fall guy in a Charlie Chaplin film. A mangy, pop-eyed dog with a curly tail wandered out of a shop house, splashed through the water and approached me. Curious, he sniffed my face, then turned, showed me his backside and walked away, no longer interested. I looked up at the banana lady, who had hurried towards me from behind her stall. She had the girth of a sumo wrestler. Bending over me with the strength of Godzilla, she and her helper scooped me up by my armpits and in one powerful sweep, had lifted me up, plunked me down and had me standing on my feet, still holding the brief-case and the umbrella. She clacked and cackled, point-ing down to the spot where the manhole was, concealed by the muddy floodwater. Now I realized why she was frowning when she saw me and why there was that miraculous path in front of me with no other pedes-trians!

Within twenty-four hours of my arrival in Thai-land, I had been baptized, rescued by a banana lady and taught a lesson – expect the unexpected and don't let it bother you when it happens. Just say "*mai pen rai!*" – it doesn't matter. When I realized nothing had been broken, we both broke into laughter. Drip-ping wet, I went back to the hotel, changed into my other safari suit – navy blue – and was picked up and driven in style to the office two blocks away. Every morning, till I moved to my house on the river, I passed the banana lady and we had a good laugh. She was the first in a collection of Bangkok charac-ters who would fill my life over the next five years. Neither of us had reached nirvana yet, but we were trying as best we could.

It wasn't long before I went from the arms of the banana lady into the clutches of my landlady, Khunying Boonlong Devarat. I had found the per-fect house just steps from the river, in a neighbor-hood more like a village than a part of the city. A charming but neglected early twentieth-century wooden structure with wide, wraparound porches and a garden crowded with mango trees, it had no hot running water nor other modern conveniences, but that didn't matter to me. It had cast a spell on me and I was enchanted by the neighborhood's Old-World atmosphere.

Now a titled "lady" (*khunying*), the owner had once been a lady of the evening. Her birth name was Soo Ling. In the 1920s, she and her sister, Soo Long, had come to Bangkok from China as teen-aged prostitutes. At that time, it was not uncommon for poor Chinese with large families to alleviate their poverty by selling one or more children for a small sum of money. Sons were sold as laborers, daughters as indentured servants, or if they were beautiful, they joined the world's oldest profession as prostitutes. Fresh off the boat, the Soo sisters had found employ in a Bangkok teahouse where they become known for their beauty and especially fair skin, smooth as porcelain, according

to one old client. Soo Ling was especially gifted; her reputation spread beyond the reaches of Yawarat (Chinatown) when satisfied customers recounted how she could play the mandolin and, at the same time, crack melon seeds with her teeth, passing them mouth to mouth to the eager recipient.

In a few years, she rose from tart to courtesan, entertaining lusty members of the highest circles, including the nobility. At that time, the king of Thailand was Vajirawut, famous as the founder of the Thai Boy Scouts and also known for his homosexual persuasions. One of his paramours was a young nobleman who also frequented the teahouses and had made the acquaintance of Soo Ling. In time, his fascination with her led to a proposal of marriage and a noble title. She left her brothel for a mansion on the river and became her ladyship, but never lost her love for a good time. In the 1930s, she became infamous in upper-crust Bangkok circles for hosting demimondaine gatherings. At one of these "salons," she fatally shot one of her suitors in an argument. The ensuing trial rocked Bangkok's high society in the days just before World War II and, as expected, led to her exoneration.

Now, forty years later, she sat in her house on the river with her memories, collected her rents and stared out the window. Her bedroom overlooked the entrance to the compound where I lived. Whenever I came home late, I could see her silhouette, a shadow puppet in the gloom, mumbling to herself in a raspy, coarse voice. Often, she would lean out her window and croak at me, telling me I shouldn't stay out so late. We only met once, when I invited her to lunch at my house. She was bent with age and resembled a withered crocodile. Her Thai was barely understandable, so thick was her Chinese accent, but her skin was still like porcelain and I could see that once, she had been beautiful. Thirty years later, when I returned to Bangkok, I ran into Lady Boonlong's ghost, but that story must wait for a while.

Early in 2003, I embarked on a nostalgic trip to Southeast Asia, touring the cities I used to know and work in. My career had gone well in spite of my inauspicious plunge down Alice in Wonderland's hole that rainy day in Bangkok. Now retired with time on my hands, I wanted to go back and see what I could find of my old life. There must be sights and sounds that would bring old memories to life again. My friends joked that I was trying to recapture the rapture of my youth by going back to the haunts of my salad days. They told me I would be disappointed and wouldn't find what I was looking for. Thomas Wolfe said you can never go home again, but I had to give it a try.

It was my first time in Bangkok in thirteen years and when I got there, I was overwhelmed with the changes I saw. Bangkok had become an urban nightmare, but somehow I hoped that time would have bypassed my house on the river a few miles north of the city's center. I needed to go back in time and find a place that hadn't changed. I remembered those years nearly three decades past and it seemed like only yesterday. I boarded the river taxi that took me up the Chao Phraya River, past the Temple of Dawn. We passed huge teak barges carrying loads of rice and tiny canoes paddled by old women selling food from smoking charcoal braziers. The muddy river swirled, carrying bunches of water hyacinth, which had drifted down from the countryside. I saw the familiar outline of the roof of my old house. It was still there! The boat lurched to a halt at the dock, punctuated by the shrieking whistle of the boat boy as he tied it to the wharf poles. I jumped from the boat to the dock and stood for a moment. Miraculously, nothing had changed. On the road leading to my old house, flower vendors were still selling their garlands of jasmine and orchids, which passers-by bought and offered at the temple nearby; merchants sitting in cool, dark shop houses surrounded by huge sacks of rice were still clicking their abacuses and smoking; school children chanting rhythmically in the temple school compound droned through the midday heat. I was on my way to meet Khun Ratawat, Lady Boonlong's son, and I wanted to visit my old home before seeing him. He had lived in the compound too. Perhaps we could share some memories of when we were both young in old Bangkok. Through mutual acquaintances, we had been in touch and I was curious to see what the old dragon's son was like. I stood in front of my old house and gazed up at the window where his mother used to perch in her roost, waiting to pounce on me. No sign of life. I guess she had passed away, probably years ago. She would have been nearly a hundred if she were still alive today. The only sound came from the river, the distant hum of boats churning up the water, the lap of the tide against the dock. It seemed so quiet, almost deserted.

How I loved the river and the life I led when I lived by it. I was always near the water or traveling on it, sometimes in a boat so small that I felt a part of the water itself. I recalled one night when I crossed the river in a tiny boat to visit the wife of a Thai friend. The boat was piloted by the old lady who always waited at the dock to take people back and forth to the other side. There were three of us beside the old lady and I thought we would surely sink as we rocked up and down in the fragile shell. Lightless and powered by a motor that sputtered fitfully, the boat made its way across the dark water and stopped in front of a house on stilts, hanging over the water. Inside the house – it was really more of a shack – was an immensely fat, old *farang* (European) lady in a shapeless gown. She was chain-smoking and speaking Thai like a market woman, punctuating her words with guttural bursts of "uuhh, uuhh!" I was told by my friends that she was English, but when I spoke to her in what I thought to be her native tongue, she stared at me blankly. I realized that she could no longer speak English, that she was no longer the person she had been. On a shelf high up in a corner, surrounded by cobwebs, was a faded photo of a beautiful young woman sitting on the terrace of a Tudor mansion, looking very proper and elegant, obviously English. She was wearing one of those elaborate hats that Englishwomen used to wear when they went to high teas or garden parties. The old woman saw me looking at the picture and steadying herself by grabbing onto nearby furniture, shuffled across the room and stood next to me. She looked at me, laughed and pointed to her face, then to the picture. Taking a drag on her cigarette, she coughed and said one word in English, "Me!" then shook her head and laughed again, turning away as she lapsed into another spasm of coughing. What was her story? How had this proper Englishwoman ended up an old hag

in a shack on a river in Thailand? Expect the unexpected, I thought. Thailand was teaching me that only Lord Buddha knew the answer to life's questions.

Pulling myself back from my reverie, I gazed again at my house and looked over the roof through the trees to the next compound with its grand buildings. That was where the close relatives of Her Majesty, the Queen, lived. I often visited the

queen's sister-in-law; entering her compound was a trip to a rarified, hidden world where people spoke in subdued voices, and rather than standing, servants crawled on the floor and served on their knees in the servile style of old-fashioned Siam. Another neighbor was Pikpan, granddaughter of King Chulalongkorn, who had modernized Thailand in the late nineteenth century. We became friends on hiking trips we both took with the Siam Society. Pikpan was fun and naughty sometimes. I remember one arduous hike up Pukadung Mountain in the Northeast. When our group had finally reached the summit, breathless and panting, there she was, already standing on the plateau, a drink in her hand, looking down at us and laughing, asking why we were so slow. It turned out, we later learned, that she had secretly hired two porters to carry her up the mountain in a sedan chair by another faster route!

Pikpan was modern and Westernized in many ways while remaining deeply Thai at the same time. She spoke impeccable Queen's English, graduated from Oxford and drank martinis. She was one of the most famous cooks in Thailand and had written books on Thai cuisine, which helped to make Thai cooking world-famous. She was also a renowned gardener and had written widely about landscaping. In a fascinating and rather gruesome historical aside, she told me that in her late grandfather, the king's court, his gardeners were often found to be stubborn creatures, more akin to buffaloes in their demeanor than humans and frequently needed punishing. The most effective punishment, she said, was to have the two culprits – there always seemed to be two of them – kneel before their superior and at his command, take turns slapping each other.

Pikpan herself said that she still found gardeners to be a stubborn breed. I remember one weekend afternoon, there was a soft rattle on my front door. I thought the breeze from the river might have caused the noise and paid no attention. A few minutes later, I walked around the porch to the front of the house and found one of Pikpan's servants sitting on the floor, waiting with a note in his hand. It was Pikpan's assistant gardener, a young farmer from Northeast Thailand. He had knocked on the door, but was afraid to disturb me by knocking again and had decided to just wait, knowing that sooner or later, I would show up. I opened the note, which started with a flowery apology for being a late invitation. Pikpan was inviting me that night to dinner at her palace. Her cook had been given the day off and she was "experimenting" in the kitchen herself and wanted some guests as guinea pigs. How charming and off-hand, I thought. And how delightful to receive an invitation from one of Thailand's most colorful personalities, the granddaughter of a king, who was also a gourmet chef and famous hostess. I hastily wrote out a reply accepting her invitation.

Later that evening, I joined some neighbors and we walked along the river to her house. Everything was perfect and the food was delicious beyond description. A brilliant hostess, Pikpan was in an expansive mood and regaled us with stories. She had imbibed a bit more than usual. Actually, she was rather drunk by the end of the dinner. She laughingly complained that she had been abandoned by all of her servants that evening, save for the junior gardener, whom she had forced to remain in the house. He moped about the kitchen with a sullen look on his face. The rest of the household had asked permission to attend a funeral and they had all taken off in a bus for the Northeast. "Bloody northeasterners!" she said. "Just like buffaloes!" Hadn't changed since her grandfather's time! Leaving her in the lurch just when she needed them the most! What they all needed was a good boxing on their ears! Servants were intolerable bores these days! Some hours and many drinks later, we said goodnight and left her as she was pouring herself another glass of wine. As I walked out the door, I heard her barking at the gardener, ordering him to bring dishes from the table to the kitchen. Outside, a cool breeze was blowing in from the river and I heard the old lady at the dock crying out *"Kam fak!"* (crossing over). Late at night, she ran a taxi service in her tiny canoe, carrying passengers to the other side of the river.

The next morning at my office, there was a buzz among the secretaries who were poring over a Thai newspaper. One of them approached me, holding up the paper and pointed to a photo saying, "You knew Mom Rajawong (royal title) Pikpan, didn't you?" She thrust the obituary at me while I read in silence. Pikpan had been strangled to death by her gardener around midnight when they were alone together in the palace after her dinner guests had left. The gardener had told the police, who captured him fleeing in a stolen vehicle, that she had forced him to work when all the other servants had been given the day off and that she had made him do "woman's work" – carry dishes and work in the kitchen, where a man doesn't belong. I thought about how gentle the Thais were. How could this have happened?

Then I realized Pikpan had committed the ultimate sin. Her behavior had been un-Thai. She had shouted at the gardener, misunderstanding him, a simple person, stripping him of the one thing he owned – his dignity. She had not respected him, telling him to do work which was shameful for a man in Thailand. She had defied the delicate social code so important in her country. Unforgivable from one Thai to another, especially from a Thai who was highborn and should have known better. If I had done the same thing, the gardener would have dismissed me with quiet contempt as an awkward, impossible foreigner who could never learn Thai customs and culture. Strange to say, and sad, I seemed to have learned more about Thai culture than Pikpan, granddaughter of a king.

The irony was that in the years I had known her, she had taught me so much about her country. On that fateful evening, she had forgotten how to be Thai, not remembering that there is often danger when East meets West and the boundaries become blurred. Even though I had come to expect the unexpected, I could not have anticipated that tragic ending to a perfect evening. And yet, in a sense, it seemed pre-destined. Pikpan had been living in a bygone era her whole life, this granddaughter of a king, who saw no need to leave her palace and live in the real world. Thailand could be a trap for those intoxicated with their own importance, unwise enough to wander astray from the accepted path, the middle way.

Looking back one more time at my old house, I boarded the water taxi and headed downriver. Khun Ratawat had asked me to meet him at the Royal Bangkok Sports Club. When I arrived there, the surroundings were much grander than I had remembered them to be. At the entrance, my humble taxi was dwarfed by sleek limousines of the very rich, who were gathering at the club for power lunches. Lackeys were everywhere, bowing and scraping. I climbed the marble stairs lined by rows of potted palms and

spotted my host. He was sitting in a rattan chair, flanked by two floozies who were fanning him. He wore his seventy-some years well, sporting a ruddy complexion framed by hair dyed shoe polish black and aviator sunglasses, whose gleaming lenses re-flected my face as I walked towards him.

Despite his macho image and expensive playboy outfit, there was something vaguely sad and down at the heels about him. Underneath the well-staged bravado, he seemed tired and resigned, a general who was no longer powerful and had no troops to command or lackeys to order about. There was no mistake about the pedigree of the young ladies. Chi-nese, in their late twenties, they squealed and pouted, calling Khun Ratawat "Daddy." They would have been considered beautiful if they had not been so coarse. Even so, their porcelain, ivory-white skin made them stand out and I thought of what my landlady, his late mother, must have looked like in her prime, when she plucked her mandolin strings and cracked melon seeds for eager suitors. Would she have approved of this scene, which mirrored her own life?

After introductions, we moved to the dining room and settled at a table, with the vixens on either side of Khun Ratawat. While we considered the menu, they fed him with their hands from silver bowls containing peanuts, screeching whenever a nut would slip through their fingers on to his lap. This caused Ratawat to display fits of mock anger, promising to spank them when they got to wherever they were going next. Their knowledge of both Thai and English was extremely limited, but I gathered they were single, liked to dance and wanted to go to the United States.

This is where I came in. I suddenly realized why I had been invited to this ludicrous luncheon. Before dessert was served, Khun Ratawat asked me if I would marry one of these charming hussies so she could get to the United States. The whole scene was so ridiculous that I found it delightful. So much for Thai subtlety and politesse. Here was the son of Soo Ling, playing out his Oedipus complex with two Chinese tarts and me, a gay man. Did he know how much his two doxies must have resembled Soo Ling and Soo Long, his own mother and his aunt? To pass the time and to relieve myself of what was becoming a fast-growing discomfort, I began to flirt aggressively with both the girls, confessing that I had a problem. I wanted to marry both of them, I said, but how could I do that? We all laughed and then got quite serious, thinking about how we could solve the dilemma.

By this time, Khun Ratawat had paid the bill and was looking conspicuously at his diver's wristwatch. He obviously wanted to blow the joint with his two bimbos. I guess the prospect of losing both of them to me was too much for him to contemplate. We said goodbye as the girls looked back, blowing me kisses. I promised to take them dancing. Then I fled in the opposite direction, in need of a stiff drink. Expect the unexpected, and don't let it bother you when it happens! Lord Buddha and the Banana Lady would have been proud of me! I descended the carpeted stairs of the Sports Club, trading its rich elegance for the heat and noise of the street. As I lifted my arm to flag down a taxi, I wondered: had I moved a few inches closer to nirvana?

CHAPTER SIX
THE GOLDEN HOUR

At first, I thought they were animals. In the gathering gloom as early evening crept in over the dockside, they appeared to be strange, mule-like creatures, straining and groaning as they dragged the creaking, overloaded wagons along the waterfront. When my eyes adjusted to the darkness, I saw that they were men, South Indians, their skin almost as dark as the night surrounding them. Nearly nude except for the rag of a dirty loincloth around their groins, hundreds of them marched, sweating and glassy-eyed like zombies, pulling primitive, two-wheel carts loaded with bricks, stones and all manner of heavy material. Emaciated but somehow still muscular, they no longer resembled humans and had become merely beasts of burden as they strained barefoot, tugging the lumbering carts over jagged cobblestones. As I drew closer, silently watching them struggle with their backbreaking loads, I heard low snorts and a steady grunting sound and was overcome by reeking body odor more akin to animals than humans. This was the underclass of Rangoon, the lowest of the low; the *kala* coolies, whose ancestors had been imported from India more than a hundred years ago to perform menial tasks too low for the native Burmese. Even buffalo and horses were too expensive to waste on the drudgery performed by these sub-humans, whose life expectancy seldom exceeded thirty years. In the old days, they had had the comfort of opium to chase away insomnia, physical pain and gnawing hunger. Now, in postcolonial times, the do-gooders had outlawed narcotics, taking away from them the one thing that made life bearable. I watched them toil until dusk turned to night; suddenly, they were no longer visible as the moonless dark swallowed these living skeletons. A breeze moved in from the water across the river bank and I breathed a sight of relief as the air was suddenly freed from the summer's stifling heat and the hideous perfume of human slaves.

It was eight o'clock and night had fallen. I had gone from the sublime to the horrible in a matter of minutes. Two hours earlier, I had witnessed what to me was the most beautiful thing in Burma, something I had never found in any other country. I called it the "golden hour," that time of day between afternoon and night when the sun begins to set and a gilded light settles in the air. Everything is bathed in gold; faces become soft and lovely, buildings look like palaces, trees turn into sculpture, the river a sea of beaten, precious metal. For a moment, only a moment, one felt as though heaven had descended on earth. The Burmese called it the time when even ugly people are beautiful.

The best place to be during those magic moments was the Shwedagon Pagoda. Perched on a hill, a towering golden spire overlooking Rangoon, the pagoda was reached by steep, covered steps which mounted majestically in all four directions: north, south, east and west. Each stairway contained hundreds of tiny shops selling jewelry, leather-bound books, bolts of embroidered cloth, religious paraphernalia, statues of Lord Buddha, saffron robes and umbrellas, items necessary for ordination into the monk-hood and seemingly endless collections of fascinating minutiae, like stuffed animals and medals which had decorated the breasts of British soldiers' uniforms. As was so often the case in Burma, music floated through the air from some undisclosed location, gossamer sounds of a harp rising as a plaintive soprano voice sang in minor key, mourning her lost love. From dawn to dusk, the pagoda was crowded with pilgrims lighting incense, its bluish plumes of smoke rising languidly before the huge image of Buddha, whose eyes stared out impassively over the throngs.

Most of the suppliants were simple people, but there were also members of the elite, colonels, generals, rich Chinese and their pampered wives, who stepped from black limousines driven by uniformed soldiers. They came to pray that their winning streaks and luck would continue to give them more of the wealth and power they now possessed. As they mounted the steps to Shwedagon, these blessed "golden" people would toss a few coins to the paupers and beggars who had strategically located themselves along the path of merit leading to the upper platform of the pagoda.

Barefoot, the worshippers circled the platform, pausing in front of one idol to light a stick of incense, then moving to another to offer a garland of jasmine. When the golden hour arrived, the worshippers' colorful silk sarongs blended with the ethereal light as their heads swayed gently while they prayed. The vanishing rays of sun caught the highlights in their shining black hair, which gleamed with the sheen of fragrant coconut oil. I had reached the riverbank too late to see the golden hour's effect on the beasts of burden. Could it have made them as beautiful as the pagoda and the golden-skinned Burmese who prostrated themselves on its cool marble floor?

As a newly arrived foreigner, I was stunned by the contrasts I experienced in Burma and the contradictions they represented. How could a benevolent Buddhist society governed by a socialist government professing belief in the welfare state allow such disparities to exist between humans living in the same city, just walking distance from one another? My interest was more than just academic. I had come to Burma as part of the "development set" to work with the United Nations in a program which aimed to provide technical assistance to the country in almost all aspects of "nation-building"– expansion of health care systems, increases in agricultural productivity, curriculum development in education, narcotics eradication, and a host of other improvements ranging from the advancement of women to environmental protection, from bee-keeping to hotel management. At the outset, it appeared that the Burmese way to socialism, as the prevailing form of government was officially called, would be a compatible partner with the UN effort to uplift the lives of the people. It seemed like a winning formula – a centralized government with unlimited authority to command what it wanted to be done, working in tandem with international experts possessing world-class knowledge and state-of-the-art management techniques. Sad to say, time has shown that this optimism was not justified and that Burma, now called Myanmar, has slipped further into inequality, despair and poverty. Why did this happen? Who can say for sure? These questions preoccupied my thoughts during the five years I was there. I'm not sure that I found the answers, or that anyone would ever solve the riddle that is Burma.

Burma sits in the cradle of what is continental Southeast Asia, an area whose cultures derive directly from the great civilizations of India and China. The richness and diversity of Indochina's culture stems from its being a blend of these two great motherlands and their primordial influences, which vary markedly when one travels from east to west.

In the eastern regions of Southeast Asia, China holds greater sway. Vietnam, especially in the north, has a distinctly Chinese flavor in nearly all aspects of its life. With the exception of the inhabitants of the

Mekong Delta, which is more an extension of the Khmer Empire, the Vietnamese closely resemble Chinese in appearance; their cooking can be described as an offshoot of China's cuisine; and their arts – music, painting, architecture, theater and language – are clearly recognizable as part of the Chinese world. Even more important, their thought patterns and attitudes are inspired by Chinese Confucian principles, the result of centuries of vassalage to their larger northern neighbor. Farther to the west, the pendulum swings in favor of India. Passing through Thailand, one notices a crescendo of Indian influences. Arriving in Burma, the traveler might well think he had come to India. That most telling of national traits – body language – is almost purely Indian. Burmese nod their heads back and forth vigorously while speaking to better reinforce a point; they punctuate their conversation with brisk backward sweeps of the hand and raise their voices to a confrontational decibel level unheard of and unacceptable in Thailand or Vietnam. Being in a teashop or a restaurant in Thailand is a world apart from a similar setting in Burma, where the cacophony of chatter is overpowering. More to the point, side by side with their natural, gentle friendliness, the Burmese personality is possessed of a type of pecking-order obsequiousness and an obsession with authority that is quintessentially Indian. It would not be an exaggeration to say that in Burma, one of the national pastimes is determining one's proper place in the human hierarchy, be it professional, social or familial, and adhering to that position tenaciously, defending one's own turf from intruders from below, as well as groveling faithfully to one's superiors and patrons above.

I learned from my years in Burma that there is an utter lack of comprehension by its people of the concept of equality in human relationships, no matter how similar two people seem to be. One example will drive home the point. After some months of working at close quarters with the local staff in our Rangoon office, I began to notice a very pronounced code of conduct, which always entailed subservience by one party and command behavior by the other. While I realized that in all societies, including the supposedly very democratic America, differences in status – be it age or position – do exist and do occasion nuances of difference in behavior, I was struck by the extremes to which this was carried out in Burma. The illustrative case in point involved the seating of passengers in an automobile. It became apparent to me within a few days of my arrival that the "shot gun" seat, that seat next to the driver, was regarded by Burmese as the undisputed place of honor for a passenger. I then noticed that one local colleague would invariably defer to another in taking this seat. Both of the people in question were "equal" as far as I could see, same job and same age, so it should have been a matter of "first come, first served" in taking that seat. It never was. I watched in amazement each time they traveled together. One man would squeeze in back of the car no matter how packed it was and the other would follow, sauntering to the front, taking the prized seat.

One day, my curiosity got the best of me and I asked them point-blank, "Ba Soe, why does Tun Win always sit in front next to the driver?" The answer was straightforward and delivered without hesitation, doubt or shame, "Tun Win is senior to me. He is two months older, one step higher in grade and joined the organization three months before I did. Very senior to me, sir." I reflected on this conversation as well as the meetings we had had in our office and how Ba Soe, far more intelligent than Tun Win, had always deferred to the latter in any decision or recommendation we were tasked to accomplish, never daring to venture his own ideas or opinion in the presence of his senior colleague.

This suffocating practice prevailed in our office among the local staff. The only way to find out what they were really thinking was to talk to them alone on a one-on-one basis. Needless to say, free exchanges and discourse based solely on facts and intelligence were also virtually absent from the corridors of government. The result was under-utilization of the best brains in the country because of the severe constraints imposed on their use by an archaic, almost medieval social structure. As time passed, I came to realize how imperative it was for the Burmese to establish their social "rank" vis-à-vis one another. A lack of clearly defined status whereby a shadow of doubt existed as to who should do what and to whom created an environment of uncertainty and stress, two conditions which Burmese cannot abide. But freedom of action, social mobility and opportunity are based largely on the flexibility and fluidity which ill-defined status often creates. A social fabric which is based on democracy and equality reinforces initiative, which is essential in seizing those opportunities that result in the movement forward which we call progress. In Burma, there could be little movement forward due to the ossified social structure, with its webs of interpersonal relationships that stifle the ability to think and act. To the regime that held sway, progress and change were considered strange and threatening.

Every day, I saw this mindless worship of authority and status played out, even in the most unlikely situations. In government offices, it was particularly annoying and counterproductive. Discussions on technical issues were severely hampered by the necessity of the Burmese at any given meeting to defer to the authority of the "senior" person present. Often, the senior member in a discussion was not a technical person at all, but a political appointee with a total lack of professional competence in the subject being discussed, who hadn't a clue about airfields or vaccines or reforestation. Still, the foreign technical experts were compelled to talk exclusively with that "senior" person while the technical staff sat silently throughout the whole meeting. If the foreign consultant made the mistake of directly addressing the person he knew to be the specialist, the unfortunate man, or in rare cases, woman, would sit mute, staring straight ahead, waiting uncomfortably for the senior person to speak. On rare occasions, the junior expert, daring to take the initiative, would bend near the boss, whispering in his ear, providing him with a face-saving answer. Open, productive discussions with give and take, not to mention meaningful decisions, were rarely realized. And so it went with meetings that were supposed to determine the destiny of a nation's development.

As individuals, Burmese were singularly indisposed to taking any action on their own and constantly sought group approval for the smallest act before committing it. I recall one evening, I needed to have a shirt ironed before I went out for an appointment. Since my housekeeper was off that day, I set to the task myself, standing at the ironing board by the window looking out on the street. It was already dark and with the additional cover of a tall hedge that bordered our compound, I could see out, but those passing by on the road could not see me. I always enjoyed being able to secretly watch passing scenes and the people who animated them, seeing the Burmese in their most natural state of behavior. As I ironed away, I heard laughs and chatter coming from the road, which was by now deserted. There were a dozen women walking in a group, returning from the nearby market with their day's purchases balanced on their heads. Suddenly, one of the women declared to the group that she had to pee. Everybody cackled and howled and teased her about this and that. It appeared that she was the only one of the bunch who had this urgent call of nature. After lengthy consultations and more laughter, all of the women squatted in unison by the side of road, lending group solidarity and approval to what would in the West be a supremely personal act carried out with a maximum of privacy. If this same situation had presented itself in the West, the needy party would simply say, "I've got to take care of something and I'll catch up." Not in Burma, where groupthink suffocated any thought of individualism.

On a personal level, this culture of seniority had its insidious effect on certain foreigners who began themselves to take on the trappings of overbearing Burmese behavior. Many older European project managers began to fancy themselves as very senior and acted in a pompous, colonial way. While the Burmese were diffident to a fault when they dealt with their own kind, it was not always the case when a Burman and a foreigner were speaking to each other. Sometimes, there were confrontations, with near-disastrous results. I remember attending a meeting at which I was supposed to adjudicate a dispute about control of a project vehicle that had been allocated by the United Nations to the Forestry Department, a Land Rover, as I recall. At issue was where it would be parked after office hours. I expected that the other participants at such a meeting would be relatively junior administrative types, given the rather petty nature of the agenda. I was more than a bit surprised when I arrived at the cavernous government compound to find the top people sitting at the conference table, glaring at each other. The expatriate chief technical advisor wanted it garaged in his compound and the native director-general insisted that it remain in the government motor pool at night. I suspected that both of these gentlemen had hidden agendas and wanted it for their private personal use in the evening. I had been given to understand that the D-G had been sighted in recent days using it to ferry his children to an exclusive private school reserved for the offspring of military brass. And when he could manage to get his hands on it the CTA was seen joyriding in the vehicle with his girlfriend.

I was stunned by the petty vehemence and severity of the discussion that ensued. It lasted for hours and descended into an argument bordering on physical confrontation. I watched as tempers rose, observing two men, one a PhD in a highly technical subject, the other a cabinet-level government official, whine and shout like schoolboys. Were they debating the fine points of a technical matter that would impact on the projects they were administering? Was this a struggle for a meeting of the minds on a nettlesome budgetary question? No, it was a matter of where four wheels would spend the night, a childish display of power. As the United Nations was the source of funding for the project, I realized that I held a bit of leverage, namely the purse strings. I ended the contretemps by telling them that neither would have it their way and that the United Nations would keep the vehicle in ITS compound.

The meeting concluded with all three parties walking away, frustrated with the outcome and unhappy with each other. Trust and understanding, so essential to development work, had reached a low ebb. As I became more familiar with the reality of the "development" profession, I realized with regret that this kind of meeting occurred all too frequently. It was symptomatic of a system mired in the past, flailing under the strictures of a kleptocratic military dictatorship. Once, prospects for the future seemed to hold great promise, but fifty years after gaining independence, it appeared that Burma's golden hour was a distant dream.

How different it all seemed on the eve of Burma's nationhood. The future looked bright when Burma left the British Empire in 1948, a year before India gained her independence. So precocious was Burma as a colonial offspring that it was deemed mature enough to pursue its own fortune as a democracy ahead of the timetable originally planned for the break-up of British India. Burma excelled in all areas of national life considered to be bellwethers for a healthy sovereign state. Its literacy rate was the highest in the colonies; the population was well-educated in crafts, skills and professions, assuring it the technical self-sufficiency required for successful functioning as a state; good governance also seemed guaranteed since its institutions were sound and well-developed; schools, colleges and universities had been turning out graduates for several generations under the tutelage of British administrators; courts, hospitals, and an effective police system guaranteed a high standard of justice, public health and law and order. In trade and commerce, Burma was a role model for other countries in the region, leading in exports, manufacturing and diversified business investment, with one of the highest standards of living in Asia. It seems unbelievable today that in the 1950s, shoppers would travel from Bangkok, Colombo and Saigon to visit the department stores and emporiums that flourished in Rangoon. Coupled with the advances that colonialism seemed to bestow on Burma were its indigenous accomplishments, exemplified by its ancient culture and the humane social environment that had been implanted by the widespread embrace of Buddhism. As both the religion of the majority as well as a way of life for the entire population, Buddhism had planted deep roots in Burmese society and had given it the traditions of charity, tolerance and loving kindness, which have sustained the country even in the difficult times it now faces.

With the best of the East and West, a seemingly harmonious blend of the old and the new, what went wrong? Why is Burma now a basket case, one of the poorest countries in Asia, classified by the United Nations as "least developed?" The answers, if there are any, can be found in bad luck and bad habits. Burmese democracy flourished for more than a decade before it was crushed by the imposition of a military dictatorship in 1960. Perhaps, the brief experiment in democracy had succeeded too well. Within months of independence, a dizzying array of political parties exploded and by the late 1950s, near anarchy seemed to prevail.

Always simmering beneath the surface, but kept in check by the British during the colonial period, ethnic strife began to eat away at the remaining political stability. Taking advantage of a fluid and unstable political environment, ethnic groups such as the Christian Karens, long restive and frustrated at not having achieved nationhood for their tribes, began open, armed rebellion against the newly created state. In a pattern now all too familiar in the postcolonial world of newly independent states, a strongman "came to the rescue," stamping out the accomplishments that had been nurtured for over a century. The new ruling clique was composed of uneducated, xenophobic military officers who had gained recognition earlier in Burma's history as freedom fighters, when they formed resistance groups against the Japanese occupiers during World War II. Searching for an ideology to replace the democratic system they had just destroyed, the generals followed what they called the Burmese Way to Socialism. This new creed was a quirky blend of Marxism, Chinese Great Leap Forward ideas about self-sufficiency and scorn for Western technology, wrapped in a cloak of Buddhist mysticism. Taking a cue from the Communists, Ne Win and his generals developed a strategy which made religion the opiate of the masses, allowing the population relatively unfettered access to religious life in exchange for an absence of political choice or economic well-being. A "let them eat cake" attitude translated into "let them have their prayer beads." As the country sank deeper into poverty and despair, the only recourse for a suffering people was to look to religion, but it became an unhealthy faith, based largely on mysticism, superstition and soothsayers. Fortunetellers became all the rage, with government ministers consulting astrologers as a matter of course before making any decision. Overnight, Burma found itself falling back into the Middle Ages, slipping into paranoid isolation, mistrusting the outside world as well as its own people. The democracy and freedom which had developed and flourished over the past century had been stamped out overnight, leaving an eerie backwater of a country whose remaining wealth and riches were systematically plundered by the new ruling class like so many vultures pecking over carrion.

How did we, the foreign community, fit into this crumbling hermit kingdom? I wondered what I was getting into when I stepped off the plane from Bangkok that February day nearly thirty years ago. Our jet, the only aircraft in sight, seemed to dwarf the tiny Rangoon "international" air terminal, a shabby remnant of 1950s Asian art deco, which stood forlornly baking in the midday heat. Just forty-five minutes before, we had been in Bangkok, a bustling city of skyscrapers and vital energy, with an airport rivaling New York or London. As I entered the terminal, I could scarcely see, so dim were the lights. Inside the somber arrival hall, there seemed to be no activity. The few people who were there stood motionless like wax museum figures, staring at me as I made my way through the gloom. The strong odor of carbolic disinfectant hit my nostrils, making me think of the loos in the London underground back in the 1950s, one of the lingering gifts of colonialism that still remained in Burma. A single ceiling fan rattled overhead barely stirring the hot, acrid air as the customs inspectors slowly perused the contents of my bags, lifting and inspecting each garment as though they were Christmas shopping at a department store. I realized these threadbare souls were admiring my possessions, hoping for a handout. Looking me in the eye as they held up each item, they seemed to say, "Won't you give me this shirt? You have so many of them." I

noticed the prosper-
ous-looking passen-
ger in front of me,
presumably a Bur-
mese returning from
abroad, handing his
passport to the official
blocking the exit
door. Tucked not so
discreetly inside its
pages were several
crisp greenbacks. An-
other sign that we
had entered the
world of Indian cul-
ture where tea

money and baksheesh, greased the wheels of daily life.
I also noticed that the Burman had walked out the door,
surrendering his passport to the immigration officer.
For its citizens, it seemed that Burma was one big jail
where the act of traveling, so taken for granted in the
United States, was not a right, but a rare privilege
granted only to the favored few.

The physical beauty of the people and the charm
of the country and its culture cast their spell on outsid-
ers, making it easy to obscure the reality that for expatriates, Burma was a hardship post. Unlike most affluent western societies where culture is either an elite,
moneyed "see and be seen" pastime or a dead-end passive exercise in watching violence, Burmese cultural
life was both refined and democratic and ran deep into
the soul of the masses of its people. Ancient, but still

the most popular form of culture, the *pwe* (performance) incorporated classical dance, music, drama, comedy and philosophy in an endless series of acts, performed in tents or out in the open air under the stars. In October after the rains had ended, these performances attracted ordinary people coming on foot from miles around, starting at night and running continuously until dawn. The entire family, carrying mats, blankets and dinner boxes, would settle in for a night of entertainment incorporating morality plays, bawdy skits, spectacular circus acts and magical music and dance. The more serious elements of the performance would be played out in the early hours of the morning, subliminally designed to penetrate the minds of the audience who had dozed off on their mats. The morning after a *pwe*, I would joke with my sleep-deprived colleagues in the office when I caught them nodding at their desks. I told them they had a "*pwe* hangover." The Burmese called it being "bitten" by the *pwe*. The remedy required many cups of strong Burmese tea to shake us from our *pwe*-induced reveries.

I found myself falling under the spell of Burma, but sadly, the attraction was unrequited. As friendly and polite as the Burmese were, there was always an invisible line that was drawn when they interacted with a foreigner. They never seemed totally relaxed and spontaneous; the look in their eyes changed when a foreigner entered the room. What was it? The decades of colonialism when the British had been the "masters" and the Burmese were taught that they were inferior? Surely that was part of the answer, but the imperialists were long gone. Perhaps, it was the intimidating physi-

cal disparity between a pale-faced, six-foot, two-hun-
dred-pound Westerner, with his big nose and red hair,
and the delicate Burmese, who felt threatened by such
a figure? Whatever the reasons, the Burmese were eth-
nocentric to the point of being racists. Not racists in
the manner of the KKK, but racists nonetheless. It was
inconceivable that one could be Burmese without having black hair and golden skin. The impossibility of being
fully accepted was for me psychologically very painful
since one can never be happy unless one is a full member of the society in which one lives. How strange it was
to live in a place but feel that I was on the outside,
looking through a glass I could never penetrate. So
eager was I to bridge this gap that I took to wearing
disguises, hats and dark glasses that would hopefully
lessen the differences and make me acceptable. But
no hat or pair of spectacles could turn me into a Burmese. At least, I had a Burmese name. I was Aung Soe
– the Sunday-born. The name had been given to me by
a carpenter who came to my apartment to build me a
beautiful teak cabinet. When we introduced ourselves,
he said he had trouble with my English name and that
I needed a Burmese one. He asked me on which day
of the week I was born, and when I replied Sunday, he
christened me Aung Soe.

Although not tall by European standards, Burmese
possessed a statuesque quality that highlighted the per-
fection of their physical proportions and was set off by
a natural beauty in their movement, especially notice-
able when they walked. When I traveled upcountry to
small villages, I used to marvel at the young women in
the markets carrying baskets of produce on their heads.

Their bearing and allure and totally unselfconscious beauty was unrivaled by any high-fashion event I had ever seen on the catwalks of Europe. Unlike most other Southeast Asian men whose delicate physical makeup often bordered on the feminine, men in Burma were more masculine in appearance and obesity in either sex was rarely seen. The Burmese sarong, worn in favor of Western dress, with appropriate variation by both sexes, set off their physical beauty to great advantage and took on a particularly sensual quality when one noticed that underwear was seldom worn. The ease with which a sarong was fastened – or unfastened – lent a subtly erotic aspect to their garments that surpassed the crudely sexual plunging necklines and bare midriffs of Western clothing. The Burmese possessed a naturally playful and flirtatious personality, which was especially engaging when it was combined with the shy politeness they displayed on meeting foreigners for the first time. They were quick to laugh and always seemed to be smiling, even when their faces were in repose and conversation flowed easily in informal situations, when Burmese were made to feel at ease. I never ceased to be amazed at the open hospitality and generous nature of the people, especially the simple people, even when the government actively discouraged, in fact forbade, fraternization between Burmese and foreigners. Countless times, I was invited to modest homes to share a cup of tea or pay respects at an altar of Buddhist statues surrounded by offerings of fruit, food and flowers, sitting on the fine woven mats that serve as seats in place of western furniture in Burmese homes.

Rangoon had that lost, Old-World quality you find

in places like the French Quarter in New Orleans, a haunted atmosphere of having seen better times. Worn wooden structures with lacey balconies predominated in the crowded sections of the old city, a museum to a bygone era where people still rode in quirky rickshaws called sidecars, looking up as they move at a snail's pace at ornate colonial buildings housing offices and government ministries, where sleepy clerks sat with their feet propped up on stacks of dusty files that hadn't been opened in half a century. Down by the river, the Strand Hotel sits like a grand and faded old lady, her white paint peeling, the bar now choked with cheroot smoke and crowded with Burmans where not so long ago, English *pukka sahibs* in white linen barked at the natives and orchestrated the fortunes of their empire.

Farther from the center of town, immense Victorian mansions dotted the emerald-green landscape, freshened by lakes and lily ponds. And everywhere, there were Buddhist temples and pagodas, their golden spires peeping through the swaying palm trees. In the early morning, just after daybreak, hundreds of monks in saffron robes, their heads shaved, and walking barefoot in a row, filed in lines like ants from house to house with their begging bowls, collecting food for the one meal they have each day. Householders hoping to make merit, waited at the door with pots of steaming rice and curry, ladling portions into the black bowls tucked into the monks' orange robes. Every Buddhist male in Burma is expected to be ordained for at least one Lenten season, equivalent in time to the four-month-long monsoon that starts in May. Unemployment and scarcity of food swelled the monasteries with monks who

would normally not have been there beyond the per-
functory Lenten period but for hunger and lack of a
job.

As foreigners, we entered this shuttered, ancient
society like sleepwalkers, eyes closed, groping as we
walked, stumbling as we clutched onto doorknobs,
searching for light and air. Most of us never found either. For the most part, the expatriates never got to
know Burma, never wandered beyond the confines of
the international club, never learned the language or
made friends with the locals, contact being limited to
servants, their government counterparts, tennis teachers and that collection of desperate Burmese females
in search of foreign husbands and a ticket out of
deadend lives and stagnation.

Among our group of expats, there were a fair share
of rascals, eccentrics and neo-colonialists singularly lack-
ing in noble ideals and professional standards. Our senior administrative officer, Rafael, a dashingly handsome Spaniard, was deeply involved in black-market
trafficking of duty-free whiskey. Several times, by chance,
I watched, unnoticed from the street, as he and his
smuggler contact loaded case after case of Johnny
Walker into a truck from the back entrance of the Diplomatic Shop. With his ill-gotten gains, Rafael would
buy Buddha images, which had been stolen from monasteries and pagodas, smuggling them to Bangkok
through the diplomatic pouch and selling them for
huge sums in the thriving market for contraband antiques. He had also developed a drug habit not long
after arriving in Rangoon. Heroin, coming from the
Golden Triangle in the Shan States or smuggled across

the border from Northern Thailand, was easily obtainable on the street and was so pure and inexpensive that it could be smoked in a filter cigarette. He was constantly offering me joysticks, perhaps hoping that I too would get hooked. I tried one once and was surprised to find that it had no effect on me. Otherwise, I might have gotten hooked as well.

When his assignment ended and he realized that he had to leave Burma and the habits and easy money he had acquired, he circulated a petition among the local staff of our office, asking that they protest his departure. His desperate tactic was considered a sad joke and he was eventually discharged from the United Nations after a run-in with the KGB in Afghanistan, where he had been posted and where he continued his smuggling and drug habits. We stayed in touch and several years later, I learned that he had moved to Thailand, where he managed to find work with a Catholic relief organization. He also continued his trafficking of religious objects. Several months after he moved there, he was murdered in Bangkok by rough-trade types who bound him with silk chords and beat him to death with bronze, antique Buddha statues from his extensive, illegal collection. The tabloid newspapers in Bangkok didn't even give him the dignity that death deserves. His nude picture was splashed across their front pages, showing him as a scarcely recognizable collection of bloody body parts. Rafael had paid with his life for violating a sacred Burmese taboo that forbade desecration of religious objects—not the first time that westerners had defied the eastern gods at their own peril. Corpses of European mountain climbers are grim testament that those who trespass in the Himalayas where only the gods should go must pay the price for their arrogant disregard of local customs and religion. The sacrosanct mystery of the East must be respected.

Another colleague, a loopy middle-aged Belgian with a wife and children, constantly pestered me to find him a girl, saying that because I spoke Burmese and was single, I must know where to find them. Not realizing that I was pulling his leg, he took me seriously one day when I suggested that he could find somebody by going to a certain remote part of town and waiting under a bridge at midnight. I gave him elaborate instructions on how to get to his assignation. The following day, he came late to the office with circles under his eyes and accosted me during the lunch hour, saying, "Where the hell was that girl?" I shrugged my shoulders and rolled my eyes and after that, he never bothered me again. Perhaps I had done him a good turn without realizing it because he soon launched into a serious study of Buddhism and meditation, informing me that his guru, a certain Buddhist monk known among the locals as a crackpot, could fly.

My neighbor in the adjoining flat in my building was Hadley-Finch, an Englishman full of puff and bluster who referred to the Burmese as "natives" and who was a senior project manager in charge of an agricultural research station in Upper Burma. Despite protests from our office, he seldom went to the research station, preferring instead to enjoy the comforts of Rangoon and the attentions of his Indian girlfriend. The interests of their host country seemed far from the minds of these highly paid members of the development set.

It would be unfair and misleading to describe all of the expatriates as misfits and flawed characters, but even those who were dedicated and hardworking were rendered less than fully effective on the job because of various distractions and the psychological isolation of being in a country which effectively practiced apartheid against its foreign guests. It was nearly impossible for us to socialize legally with Burmese. In order to do so, the persons concerned had to submit a request to the Ministry of Foreign Affairs for permission to meet weeks in advance of the event, detailing why the contact was being made, where it would take place and who would be there. In practice, the only contacts outside of work were of a very spontaneous or furtive nature. I remember being privy to a circuit of "underground" parties, where educated young Burmese from affluent families would fraternize with their foreign counterparts in walled villas with curtains drawn. There was a certain excitement in these illicit soirees and other chance encounters, but after several years, leading a double life took its toll on Westerners, who were more used to an open society without the taboos and secrecy inherent in Burma.

Intrigue always seemed to be in the air when I lived in Rangoon. As a neutral country, Burma welcomed diplomatic representation without discrimination and virtually every country in the world was there, with a particularly heavy presence from what was then called the Eastern Bloc. Rumors were rampant about the huge Soviet complex and what went on inside. It was said that there were gorgeous Russian minxes who were planted to seduce the Marines guarding the American Embassy, as well as other enemies. In five years, I never saw one of them, but I did make the acquaintance of a number of dumpy diplomatic *babushkas* who were always near the buffet table during the Fourth of July banquet at the American Embassy. The American ambassador at that time was a colorful character who had a peg leg and a penchant for bourbon. After a few drinks, he looked more like Long John Silver than Washington's envoy, careening through the crowds with a wide grin on his face. At one point, I was approached by some intelligence types who asked me to do a little "work" for them. They proposed that I should host a series of parties at my home, where the liquor would flow freely and the guest list would include such exotic types as North Koreans and Bulgarians. I was never quite sure what was to be accomplished at these soirees – defection? The spilling of state secrets? While the idea sounded rather exciting, I never got around to hosting such an event since my idea of fun centered more on Burma and things Burmese rather than entertaining a crowd of smelly people with steel teeth.

Health was also a constant concern in Burma. There seemed to be a variety of maladies and diseases that one had never encountered or even heard of in the West, especially for those of us who were adventuresome or careless when it came to eating local food without precaution. In my third year, I came down with a bizarre ailment called *kenari yoga* or "dancer's disease," so named because of the huge carbuncles which sprouted in my armpits, forcing me to hold up my arms with elbows raised and bent like a Burmese classical dancer in order to avoid extreme pain and prevent the explosion of the festering boils. Later I succumbed to hepatitis, requiring six weeks' hospitalization in Bangkok. There was always the ongoing problem of worms, sometimes long, sometimes short ones, or round and wiggly ones. I was young, single and not particularly bothered about my physical well-being, as is often the case with youth, but medical concerns were a hindrance to many of the other older foreign technical staff, who seemed to be so preoccupied with their own physical conditions that they could talk of nothing but doctors, clinics and the need to avoid anything "local."

Observing the problems of foreigners in third-world countries and their inability to adjust to local conditions, a colleague of mine once suggested that the solution to meaningful, more effective foreign-aid interventions was to offer lower salaries to aid workers, thereby attracting a more grassroots type of person with a volunteer's perspective and a spirit of adventure; the kind of person who was not interested in having a chauffeur-driven car or replicating suburban American life in the Asian tropics. Even that type of person would have difficulty in a country like Burma, which seemed to want a foreign presence but did not know how to deal with it when it had arrived. The Burmese have always been plagued with a split personality when it comes to the outside world. They seem to feel that what is foreign is better, that a white face knows more than a brown one. At the same time, they are xenophobic and mistrustful of new ideas and unfamiliar situations. In the final analysis, they are the only ones who can solve their problems and realize the golden hour they so richly deserve.

CHAPTER SEVEN

SEVENTY-TWO STEPS

Berkeley, California, 1952

Funny, climbing the seventy-two steps to our house, I always thought about life and death, about how long I had left on this planet, things like that. I was fixated with the number seventy-two even before I read that seventy-two years was the average life expectancy of the average American male in 1952. That meant that

I had forty more years to live. But who believes statistics? Bob said they could lie just like people, that you could twist numbers to say whatever you wanted them to say. Bob had strong opinions about everything, including me and the way he thought I should talk and act and think, but that's neither here nor there at this point in my story. This IS a story, by the way. I'm not sure where it will lead so I'll just ramble on and we'll see what happens. Bob was always taking me places and teaching me things. He told me I had so much to learn, that there was a big, wide world out there and that I needed to be more sophisticated. We had gone to a fortuneteller in Oakland the day before my previous birthday and she had told me that I would live to be quite old. When I asked her what that meant and if I would live beyond seventy-two, she just smiled, looked at me, gazed at her cards and said, "You'll live to be as old as you want to be." Bob grumbled that she was giving me typical fortuneteller blah-blah and didn't want to pay her the five dollars advertised on her door, but I liked her answer. He laughed and tousled my hair and told me I was a hayseed who would believe anything anybody said.

As I was saying, there were seventy-two steps. It took us a long time to establish that number. After we bought the place, I counted each time I climbed them and every time, the number turned out different. I got seventy the first time, then it went up to seventy-two, then back down to seventy-one. Bob always got a higher number than I did. I said that was because he counted the ground on top when he had finished the stairs and that didn't matter. You were only supposed to count the wooden steps. We used to argue and laugh about it. Once I challenged him to walk up with me step by step and count together, but halfway up, he started clowning around, counting in Chinese and Spanish and I don't know what all languages and we broke up in stitches of laughter, rolling off the steps down the hill in each other's arms. I remember how we laid there in the tall, fragrant grass, sweaty and out of breath, looking up at the sky. The clouds seemed to be zooming by at a thousand miles an hour. I turned my head and it rested on his arm, my cheek buried in his flesh; as I blinked, my lashes brushed the golden hair on his body. I thought about what the fortuneteller had told me and knew that I wanted to live forever if Bob was by my side.

About those stairs, it finally got settled when the girls, Roni and Mikki, came over. They both got seventy-two and the next time we counted, that's what it was. And it was that same number forever afterwards. Almost as though somebody had played a trick on us and removed a couple of stairs just to give us grief. Or maybe because in those early days, we were so much in love – with life, with each other – that doing something sensible like counting was just beyond us. It seemed like we had always lived there, high up in the Berkeley Hills, above the tree line.

That's where my life began. It was a world apart; just the two of us floating in a stratosphere, far from the madding crowds below. We were so secluded that on summer days, when the sun was burning hot, we didn't even bother putting our clothes on. We'd be working out in the yard or replacing a shingle up on the roof of the barn – we called the house a barn because that's what it was when we bought it – and about noon, there would be a warm breeze from the bay, scooping up the fresh smell of the sea and adding a dash of tangy eucalyptus as it traveled up the dry hills through the big, old trees. You could almost see that breeze and feel its arms envelop you as it moved on up the hills and over the ridge to the desert. I used to stop whatever it was I was doing and just look at Bob. He was so beautiful and strong. The wind would toss his hair around and he would push it out of his eyes and just keep on working. Nothing ever seemed to faze him. He was a workhorse and used to tease me about being a dreamer. Once he looked up and saw me just sitting there on the deck, gazing at him. I can still see him and the way he looked with that half-exasperated, half-amused look on his face, saying to me, "Jim, ole boy, Rome wasn't built in a day, but if you had been part of the construction crew, it would never have got finished!" Then he laughed and threw a pinecone at my head and I went back to work, ashamed that he had caught me in my worshipful spying.

New York City, 2003

It's funny about total happiness. Looking back now on those days in the sun, I can't remember many details about our life in Berkeley. Sure, I know I'm getting old. Passed the four-score mark a couple of years ago, leaving those seventy-two steps behind in the dust. But it's more than that. Our years together were so beautiful. Being with Bob was a religious experience, an exquisite blur, like one of those sunsets over the Arizona desert or a flock of birds flying high in the sky. You can't divide up things like that and say this part was like this and that part was such and so. It just doesn't work with beautiful things, things that are so perfect. So I guess what I'm left with after all these years is a feeling and a couple of images, like Bob's face screwed up in that exasperated grin the time he threw the pine cone at me. When I close my eyes and think back, it feels like he's here in the room with me. Sometimes, his face is so close and so clear I start to speak to him. Then I catch myself after a few words and have a good laugh at the old man talking to himself. It's late afternoon. I'm sitting here alone, looking out at the Hudson River. Haven't turned on the lights yet and the apartment's getting dark. Little specks of dust float about the room like naughty gremlins. No wonder, I haven't cleaned the place in thirty years! My friend Sam tells me I'm turning into a recluse like Howard Hughes. I prefer to view myself as being in dignified withdrawal, detaching myself from worldly concerns, letting go, standing back while the rat race careens by me on its way to nowhere. Going to hell in a basket, that's what my mother used to say the few times I ever saw her. It's January and the wind rattles my windows, not like that gentle breeze that used to caress us when we were young together; when we worked and argued and laughed and made love in the sunshine up in the Berkeley Hills. I wonder where Bob is now. Good chance he's not alive anymore. After all, he was five years older than me. That would make him eighty-eight this April 25.

Berkeley, California, 1962

Late afternoon. Roasting hot outside, so hot and dry you thought you were in an oven. Everybody was talking about going to the beach after work. Somebody muttered something about forest fires. I was sitting at my desk in the library, the library at UC Berkeley where I worked as assistant librarian for the Asian collection, Japanese acquisitions, to be more exact. It was Friday and for once, my mind was more on the weekend coming up than the job in front of me. Don't get me wrong, I loved my work and wouldn't have traded what I was doing for anything in the world. It was just that events were piling up and big things were about to happen. By that, I mean anniversaries, double anniversaries. That Saturday marked the date when Bob and I met twenty years ago. It was also the tenth anniversary of our moving into the house. We hadn't planned anything special, but I knew something was cooking. Rest assured, when Roni and Mikki were involved – and they were involved because they introduced us – there would be a big to-do. A "surprise" party. What preoccupied me as we were closing up was how I could act surprised when I really wasn't. I guess the best way was to say nothing and just let my jaw drop. Oh well, *que sera, sera*; I'd do the best I could to pull off a surprised look.

At least I didn't have to worry about a present for Bob. I had been thinking about that for months. What do you give to a guy who has everything? A guy who never likes his birthday presents or what people give him for Christmas? I decided to give him something I had made with my very own hands. A ceramic vase. Last year, I had taken a course in Japanese pottery making and had become quite good at it, if I do say so myself. Forget what I say; other people used to rave about the pots and urns I made. I had set up a wheel in the barn. Luckily, Bob didn't pay much attention to me when I was indulging in my little hobby. He thought my interests were a bit eccentric and removed from reality. Pottery? Why not golf instead? You meet more people that way! He could never see that I didn't want to meet more people – that my world was complete. That I didn't want anything to change. He always teased me about learning Japanese and badgered me about why I hadn't learned French or some other "sophisticated" language instead. It never occurred to me to point out to Bob that Japanese was my bread and butter, that I got paid a good salary for knowing the lingo. It was always that way between us. He knew best and I accepted what he said like a child even when I knew he might be wrong.

The vase was the most beautiful thing I had ever made. It was a pale-green celadon color and shaped like a teardrop. I knew he would like it. Even if he didn't, he couldn't say it wasn't sophisticated. Useless word, "sophisticated"; just substitute "phony" and you've got the same thing. I guess that's what my mother tried to be, sophisticated. In one-horse Sacramento, trying to be sophisticated. "In the land of the blind, a one-eyed man is king," my father used to tell her when she'd put on airs. They ran a hotel and lived on the top floor. Sometimes I stayed with them, but most of the time, I boarded with an old woman near my school. Whenever I met my parents, they would look at me as if I were a stranger, not their son. I didn't feel as if I had any parents. I often wondered if I were really their child. The only thing I ever remember my mother saying to me was, "Run along, just now we're busy. Go find something to do with yourself." I never really had a father till I met Bob. But he was more than a father; he was everything to me. On the bottom of the vase, I had inscribed our initials with the J and the B intertwined. I got a card and some rice paper to wrap it in and I was working on a haiku, a short Japanese-style poem, to inscribe on the card. I had only written the first line, which went, "Twenty years ago . . ." I was waiting for some inspiration to finish the other three lines.

It was quarter to five, fifteen minutes before quitting time. "Quittin' time!" I sounded like some kind of clock-watching factory worker. I was jolted out of my reverie by the jangle of the phone. The voice on the other end of the line was Rose, our next-door neighbor. There was an edge in her voice and she sounded like she was choking. She spoke against a background of noise that sounded like sirens and said, "Something's happened. Get up here as quick as you can. The house is on fire." She didn't say whose house, but I guessed it must have been ours. I raced out to the parking lot and jumped into the VW. What could have happened? We had both left the house at 7:30 that morning and everything seemed fine. I didn't have a cigarette till I got in the car so I couldn't have started it by smoking. Anyway, I was always careful with my weeds. Whenever I finished a butt, I held it under the faucet and then threw it down the toilet. No way I could have started a fire. As I drove towards the hills, I saw clouds of smoke rising from the trees. The closer I got, the thicker it was.

When I got to the bottom of the seventy-two steps, there were two fire trucks, their hoses trained on the house. Or what was left of it. I stood there speechless until a fireman approached and asked me, "Is this your house?" I nodded silently as the flames continued to consume the barn, taking the roof down in a crashing spiral of sparks and smoke. By six o'clock, the house was leveled. The fire trucks had exhausted their water supply and with the danger of other fires in the neighborhood, the Fire Department couldn't send any back-up engines. It was all over in less than two hours.

I thought of Bob. No way to call him. He would be on the road now between the office and home. The only thing I could do was wait. My mind was racing like a roadrunner. What would he say? I couldn't bear for him to see our place in ruins. I thought of driving down to the junction where our road met the highway and waving him down. I'd tell him I'd made reservations at a restaurant in Berkeley and that there was no need to go home just yet. He could follow me in his car and then when we got to the restaurant, I'd figure out what to say to him about the house. The fire trucks had left and Rose gave me a hug, mumbling, "It'll all be all right, honey. You'll see." She walked away, turning back to blow me a kiss.

The only thing left was the steps. The seventy-two steps. Alone, I sat on the bottom step and looked out into space, seeing nothing. Suddenly it got cool; the weather had changed abruptly, as it often did when the wind swept up from the Golden Gate Bridge, bringing dampness and wisps of fog. I turned and walked up the steps, counting each one deliberately. Yes, there really were seventy-two of them.

When I got to the top, I surveyed the ruins. It was a sea of ashes and charred pieces of furniture. Our cook stove rose like a volcanic island from the rubble and blackness; my pottery wheel was blistered and the slabs of clay had been burnt like steaks left too long on the grill. I moved to the corner of what had been our house and my foot met something hard, almost tripping me. I looked down and saw a patch of pale green in the smoldering debris. The teardrop celadon vase I had made for Bob. I picked it up and then dropped it quickly as it burned my fingers. Luckily, it landed on a pile of ashes that cushioned the fall. I took the hand-kerchief out of my back pocket and wrapped it around the vase, taking it out to the damp grass in front of the house. It had not been damaged. I turned it upside down and blew away the ashes. The initials "J" and "B" were still there intertwined like arms embracing one another. I put the warm vase to my cheek and moved down the steps to the car. I sat down in the driver's seat and gripped the steering wheel with both hands.

I guess time had passed quicker than I imagined. There was Bob standing over me, looking first at the hill where the house had been and then back at my face. Our eyes locked and my lips trembled. I reached out and grabbed his hand as his body collapsed against the car, heaving and sobbing in gasps so heavy I thought he was struggling for his last breath. I pried my hand loose and managed to open the door and get out of the car. I came round and held him, leading him back to the steps. We sat there until darkness fell. Then we drove in my car to Roni and Mikki's. Bob was silent all the way, just staring straight ahead through the windshield at the headlights on the road. I knew that conversation was futile at that point. Anything I could say would be useless or stupid. Somehow, I was worried that Bob would blame me for the fire. I knew he wouldn't do that, but I was so afraid that this disaster would come between us. What a stupid thought, I said to myself.

We spent the night with the girls and they told us we could stay with them as long as we needed to. The next morning, I called into the library and told them I needed a couple of days off. They said they understood and told me to stay away as long as I had to. There were things to take care of. I had to go to the police and the fire department. There would be some questions and paperwork. The cops were always on the lookout for arsonists. No problem with that, I thought. It was only then that I realized we had no insurance. We had talked about getting it from time to time, but never did. It was one of those things like writing a will or paying taxes. You just didn't do it until you had to. But in this case, when we had to, it was too late. The next week was living hell. It got so bad that I couldn't answer the phone. There were so many sympathy calls; friends and friends of friends calling to say how sorry they were. One woman whom we scarcely knew called up to say that she had been invited to our surprise party and arrived at the house to find it still smoldering a day after the fire.

We stayed with the girls, but scarcely spoke a word to each other. The only thing that kept me sane was going to work. When I got back to the girls' house, Bob would be there sitting in the kitchen, drinking bourbon. When I tried to start up a conversation, he would stare straight past me as if I wasn't there and then get up and walk out of the room. Why was he doing this to me? I knew he wasn't himself and I knew the reason. But the fire had been tough on both of us, not just Bob. I was suffering too, but I knew we could get over it because we still had each other. Where was the Bob I had known and loved for twenty years? He had always been the strong one, leading me down the right paths, showing me the finer things of life, teaching me how to be sophisticated. Nights were the hardest. We used to lie there in bed and when I started to speak, Bob would cut me off and say, "It doesn't matter, it's all gone, everything we had, everything we lived for."

After a couple of weeks, we moved out and rented an apartment near the university. That was good for me because I could bike or even walk to the library. One morning, as we were getting ready to go our separate ways, him to the city to his office and me to the campus, I said jokingly to Bob, "Well, things didn't turn out so bad, did they, buddy? At least, now I can walk to work!" He glared at me in stony silence with a look that could kill and as he snatched his keys from the table, he curled his lip and snarled, "Dumb Dumb, you can say the stupidest things." That night, he didn't come home till around four in the morning. I heard him stagger in and collapse on the couch, where he remained till daybreak.

The following Tuesday was Bob's birthday. I had bought a little cake and stuck one candle in it. We had dinner later when he got home and after I lit the candle on the cake, I brought out a box and handed it to him, saying, "Happy birthday, my love." He opened the box and pushed the rice paper aside. There was the green celadon teardrop vase I had rescued from the fire. He held it up for a second, and suddenly shouted at me, "What is this piece of shit? Are you still wasting your time with that goddamn pottery crap?" He stood up, brushed past me and hurled the vase into the sink, where it landed, smashing into a dozen pieces. Now it was my turn to go out. I left the flat and didn't come back for two days. I wasn't angry, just confused. I felt like the stupid schoolboy in a Charles Dickens novel who was told he was bad but didn't know why.

I knew I was losing Bob, that he was falling and I didn't know how to catch him. When I came home early Friday morning, Bob was leaving for work. I walked up and hugged him, putting my face in his neck. He stood limp, not returning my embrace. I told him we couldn't go on like this; it was killing both of us. We had to put the past behind us. We could build another house, bigger and better, on our old lot. The old house wasn't so great anyway, was it? I said. Remember how sometimes we used to complain about living in an old barn? Let's start over, just you and me like it was before. Bob stared at me with that cold look I had grown used to of late and walked out the door. And so it went for weeks and weeks. Two strangers living in the same house, sharing the same bed, seldom speaking to each other. Bob's drinking turned serious and I never saw him sober. I wondered how he functioned at the office. He had a PR job with the airlines and had to deal with people and be charming and bright and quick. I guess he just started drinking after work and passed out and slept it off and repeated the same thing day after day.

I talked to Roni and Mikki and some of our other friends. They suggested treatment and counseling. One night, when Bob came home and before he got too deep into the sauce, I asked him if he would seek help and get some treatment. I told him I would go with him and we could make it as a team. Again I got the cold stare. Speaking before I thought of the consequences, I blurted out, "Bob, I love you, but since the fire, life has been living hell. You're not the person I used to know. What has happened? Tell me what I can do." He sat there without saying anything for a minute. I prayed that my comments had broken the ice and that his silence would be followed by a flood of apologies and promises to start over again. He opened his mouth and in a barely audible whisper, said to me, "If you don't like it, get out." I thought of our twenty years together, the seventy-two steps, those days in the hot sun laughing and loving in our own private paradise. The promises and vows we had made to love each other forever and ever, come what may. Better than a real marriage, Bob used to say, because we really believe it and don't need some preacher to tell us how to love and cherish in sickness and blah blah.

I went in the bedroom and picked up my empty suitcase. It felt like lead. Then I sat on the bed for a minute and buried my face in Bob's pillow, smelling his smell. I chocked back a sob and reached into the chest of drawers, throwing the few belongings I had into the suitcase. When I came back to the kitchen, he was still sitting there at the table, staring out into space. I put my hand on his shoulder, then raised it and gently tousled his hair like he used to do to me when we were at home on the hill. Then I bent down and pressed my lips into his curly head and whispered, "Goodbye, my love, you'll always be my guy." Without looking back, I walked out the door and got into my VW and drove away.

Kyoto, Japan, 1965

I entered the crowded subway and gazed at the sea of black hair that topped the tightly packed bodies being wedged into the car by the uniformed pusher with his nasty little wand, poking till the last arm or leg had been forced behind the doors. Packed like sardines below this foreigner, standing six foot two inches like a giant towering over his impassive flock of sheep, the Japanese never ceased to amuse and amaze me; I guess the feeling was mutual, perhaps, for opposite reasons. What was it about these people that was so different from the world I had come from in California? Words came to mind, like resigned, submissive, unresisting, patient, polite. The Japanese were all of these, but there was something more that I couldn't put my finger on. Was it inner strength? The fatalism of an ancient race? I guess that's the dilemma that most Westerners face when they go to Asia and why they end up, for lack of a better description, calling Asians inscrutable and the place they live in the "Mysterious East." Make no mistake about it. The Japanese might appear to be passive, standing in the rush-hour subway car like lambs being led to the slaughter, but that outward sign should never be taken for weakness. I had already learned in my three years there that these people had nerves of steel and an iron will. I hoped some of these traits would rub off on me.

I had left Berkeley in the fall of 1962. It was almost as though I didn't know what was happening, that I was following some distant orders handed down to me from I don't know where, but six months after the fire, I found myself on a boat heading across the Pacific to Japan. It had all happened so fast. After the fire and my break-up with Bob, what had been a charmed life seemed to take the wrong road and everything turned sour. Even the library, which had been a haven I could escape to during those months of hell, became a nest of intrigue and backstabbing. I was flabbergasted one morning when I ran into my boss, Hannah, who had always been so friendly and supportive. Her face was cold and expressionless, free of the warmth it registered every time we met. Without even greeting me, she blurted out, "Jim, you're playing a dangerous game." When I looked at her for an explanation, she muttered, "You know what I mean," and walked on.

I was stunned. She had been particularly kind after the fire. I knew my work was good, so good that the position I occupied had been created especially for me. Hannah had told me a hundred times that I had a rare mix of talents and that she never wanted to lose me. The same day, I was approached by Suzuki, a librarian scholar-in-residence on exchange

from the University of Sendai in northern Japan. His year was up and he was packing to go back home. We had become pals during his time at UC Berkeley; I helped him get settled in and he helped me with my Japanese. He said it was getting so good that he thought I was ready for the big plunge, that I ought to go and live in Japan, where I could become really fluent. I knew it was the only way. If I was to succeed in my career as a Japan specialist, I needed total immersion. Suzuki also said that he could create a job for me in Sendai, which would involve teaching English to the faculty and staff.

I guess without knowing it, I had been looking for an out and a way to leave a place that had gone from being all good to mostly bad. Roni and Mikki said I was crazy to walk away from a secure job at a world-class university. They told me I should dig my heels in and fight whatever it was that seemed to be eating away at my reputation; that I had to get to the bottom of it. Somehow, I just didn't have the stomach for a fight. If there had been two of us, if I had

had Bob behind me, if I knew I had somebody to go home to, maybe I could have done it.

Alone now, I seemed to follow the path of least resistance in everything I did. I handed in my resignation and bought a one-way ticket for Yokohama. Suzuki said he would make all of the arrangements and would even send somebody down from Sendai to meet my boat. At least, somebody seemed to want me. The day before I left, Hannah came into my office. Her expression had changed; so had the sound of her voice. She said she had been the victim of a vicious, petty plot, or rather, that I had. She begged me to withdraw my resignation and stay. As much as I knew that it might be the practical thing to do – after all, I was forty-two years old now and sacrificing my career to go off on a lark to Japan to polish up my language might not be the wisest of moves – I thanked her for her gesture, but told her I had to move on. Although I didn't articulate it to Hannah or even to myself at that point, I had reached a turning point in my life and I knew that I could never look back to anything or anybody.

By year two, Sendai began to wear thin on me. My language had grown by leaps and bounds, but the social side of my life was a dead end and a straitjacket. Being one of only five *gaijin* (foreigners) living in Sendai at the time, I felt I was under a microscope. I couldn't go anywhere or do anything without somebody coming up and telling me about it the next day. I knew it was time to move on. Besides, the job I had didn't pay me enough to survive and I was starting to eat into my meager savings. Actually, I had almost wiped out my nest egg, which didn't amount to much in the first place. I had never heard from Bob about what happened to the property on the hill. If he sold it, I knew I should be getting half the price, but I hadn't told him where I was going and I didn't have the heart to try to find out what he had done.

The wheel of fortune spun my way once again. In the spring of '65, I got an offer I couldn't refuse. An old Berkeley pal whom I had stayed in touch with wrote me that he was opening an English school in Kyoto and would I like to join as one of the founding faculty members. I was flattered and knew I had to accept, but I was a bit reluctant at the same time. After all, I wasn't an English teacher by training. Sure, I spoke English and could even conjugate a verb or two, but ESL – English as a Second Language – was a science as well as an art, with its own special methodology and structure. You could say I had been teaching English in Sendai, but what I was really doing was practicing conversation with some students; that was only one aspect of the ESL game. Ray told me not to worry about it. He said I was a born teacher and, most important, I had that empathy, the right *kimochi* (mood), which is so important to the Japanese. By that, I guess that he meant I was not an overbearing, threatening type of person. Actually, I am shy; people have been telling me that since kindergarten. I remember Bob saying I had to get out of my shell. But I think that is what attracted him to me in the first place. So maybe, being shy is not the negative we are taught it is when we grow up in America.

I was learning that "give 'em a firm handshake and look 'em straight in the eye" was just what the Japanese didn't like. And I had never liked it either. I was beginning to see that it was possible to be strong without being overbearing, that life need not be about a triumph of the strong over the weak, as we had been taught in the West. I was starting to feel at home over here even though I stood out like a sore thumb, being a *gaijin*.

I guess a new broom sweeps clean. Ray was right; my misgivings about going into teaching were unfounded. Not only did I like it a lot, I also felt I was making a contribution to the school and the students. The '60s were still very much postwar in the sense that the Japanese had not yet recovered from their defeat. The economy was booming, but the psychological trauma of losing had been hard for them to take and they hadn't come out of their shell. Learning English was one way for them to join the world again.

At first, I made some waves, which were not appreciated by the more traditional members of the faculty. Teaching English had always been very English, if you know what I mean. Very British. And that's the way it started out at our school. "Do you usually take your tea at five and would you like it served in the parlor?" type dialogue was not my style and I was able to convince Ray and some other colleagues that we had to be more modern, that we needed to have all sorts of accents – Aussie, Southern USA, Irish, and whatever else we could find – to meet the needs of a changing world.

I also got in a tangle about pronunciation, but I ended up winning that one too. Our students were really hardworking, but usually ended up on the short end when it came to conversation and comprehension. I remember one class where I sat with another American teacher and we invited a Japanese participant to join in on a conversation with us. She was lost because she couldn't pick up on the colloquial manner of everyday speech we were using. "Do you want to go?" sounded very different when spoken. It came out more like "Jew wanna go?" I started teaching colloquial pronunciation and the students really picked up on it. Before long, we were the most popular school in Kyoto.

Life was good and I found myself thinking I could spend the rest of my life in Japan. I had found a beautiful little house, I had a nice circle of friends; my job was easy and fun. That was in the early years. By the time I had been there just short of ten years, I began to experience a change of heart. I noticed that some of the other old-timers in the foreign community felt the same way too. What started bugging me was always being reminded of my foreignness. Most of the time, especially in the first few years, it seemed to be an advantage, always being deferred to, always being the center of attention, being somebody extra special.

But then, I found myself starting to crave anonymity, just wanting to fade into a crowd for a change. When I went back to California, I remember the relief of just being able to melt into the scenery on the street. I was getting tired of being stared at! I know that teachers are always on stage, but I felt that my life was turning into one big performance, that I was an object of curiosity, almost a circus clown. My age began to bug me too. The day I turned fifty, I thought to myself: How much longer can I stand in the spotlight? It dawned on me that I still had a profession that I had been trained for and had abandoned, in theory at least, only until I had perfected my Japanese. Now that I had accomplished that goal, maybe it was time to shift gears and go back to being a librarian.

Fortune smiled on me once again. I had kept up contact with the world of librarians, a fairly tight-knit community. It turned out that Columbia University was looking for a librarian for their Japanese Department and some of my friends thought that I would be a good candidate. I was told it was not an easy job. There were some prima donnas in the library and the technical staff I would be supervising were very sensitive about taking orders from a newcomer. The job needed somebody who knew how to wear kid gloves, but be firm at the same time. They asked me to come to New York for an interview.

I flew into JFK and took the bus to Port Authority. When I got off the bus, I wanted to turn around and go straight back to Tokyo. I guess I wasn't ready for the seamy side of New York City. I had never seen such dirt and poverty and roughness. I had come to New York once before in the 1950s, when Bob and I were on a busmen's holiday with the airlines. That was before my library days. We both worked for Pan Am and were given a free round trip from San Francisco.

Somehow, the gritty side of the Big Apple had escaped me until that interview trip. I decided to tell them that I wouldn't take the job. I even thought of just telephoning and canceling the interview. I couldn't find the number so I hopped a cab to the Upper West Side. We drove through Central Park and I started to realize that New York City is really a collection of different cities. By the time the cab dropped me off at the university, I had changed my mind again. The interview went well and they offered me the job.

New York City, 1972

The farewell parties were endless and I thought I would never get away from Japan. Leave-taking in Asia is a serious matter and takes time. Just like getting to know people takes longer, saying goodbye is full of ceremonial emotion, speeches, promises to meet again and lots of drinking. Then, there was all my stuff. Going to the flea markets nearly every weekend, I had become a real pack rat, with a collection of books and maps and all manner of things Japanese and Chinese. I realized with a laugh that I wasn't just a backpacking English teacher anymore, and that as an Ivy League librarian, I had "perks." I could take all this junk back to the States at somebody else's expense. Now it's all here, crammed into my apartment overlooking the Hudson River. I remember that last day in Kyoto. Somehow, I managed to be alone and found the time to climb to Yamashuri Shrine, a little Buddhist temple I had discovered on my first week in Kyoto. It was my favorite place, one of the few locations in a crowded city where you could find the solitude we Westerners craved. It was early autumn and the leaves on the delicate Japanese maples were starting to change. I mounted the old wooden steps and began to count as I climbed. For some reason, I had never counted before. Sixty, sixty-five, then seventy. There were two more steps left. Seventy-two steps. I thought how far I had come in twenty years and how long ago it was that Bob and I had climbed those stairs in Berkeley.

Berkeley, 1982

It felt like old times again. Almost. Roni and Mikki were still in their same place off Union Avenue. I had gone out to visit them during spring break and we were sizing each other up. They said I hadn't changed and I thought I better tell them the same thing even though they had each put on about forty pounds and had gone silver. They told me that Bob was still around and that he had finally gone into rehab and had been on the wagon for nearly ten years. They asked me if I wanted to see him because somehow, he had heard that I was in town and had told them he wanted to get together. I avoided answering their question because I was torn between wanting to see him and needing to forget the past. What could we say to each other after all these years? I probably wouldn't look good to him anymore, and God knows what he looked like. Roni picked up on my mood and moved quickly to another subject. The next day, when I was alone in the house, the phone rang and it was Bob. He said he wanted to meet me and suggested dinner that night. We could go to the old place in Emeryville we used to like, he said. After what seemed like a long silence, I heard myself saying that I would meet him at eight that evening.

When I got to the restaurant, he was already waiting. We shook hands and sat at a corner table. Although he had grown older, he was the same old Bob. We engaged in small talk and I talked mostly about Japan and how it had been. He told me that he had moved up in the world professionally and that he had never gotten together with anybody else. I said that pretty well described my situation too. Then he reached into the briefcase he had placed under the table and brought out a brown paper bag. He smiled and passed it across the table to me. I opened it and there was the green celadon vase I had made for our anniversary twenty years ago. It had been repaired with lumps of Elmer's glue, the syrupy brown clumsily joining the jagged pieces into a crazy patchwork that scarcely resembled the original vase. "I put it back together," he said. I smiled and took one of the daisies from the arrangement on the table and stuck it into the vase. When I released my hand to let it stand alone, it toppled over and rolled off the table onto the floor, landing with a crack and breaking into a dozen pieces. Bob stooped to pick up the pieces, but I took his arm, restraining him. "Let it be, Bob, what's done is done." He sat back down and we looked at each other until the waiter interrupted our silence. After dinner, we walked out to the parking lot to our cars, then said goodbye. The night was full of stars and a full moon lit up the Berkeley Hills. I looked out into the distance. Was it my imagination? Or did I see our seventy-two steps climbing up to the sky?

CHAPTER EIGHT
HOW DIK DIK GOT HER MOJO BACK

Dik Dik could still hear the women's voices rising over the sound of the river water as she climbed the hill back to the village. The load of wet laundry grew heavier with each step and she paused to shift its weight, repositioning the pan holding the clothes, which she balanced on her head as she walked. Turning for a second, she looked down the ravine at the other women squatting on the rocks by the water's edge, slapping the wet, foaming garments on the boulders as they gossiped. The "wop-wop" sounded like somebody getting a good spanking. The louder the slaps, the more they shouted. Their yelling rung in her ears and made her want to push them all in the river and be done with it, the silly cows.

Lucky for Dik Dik, she had finished first and could leave them to their silly nattering; her load was lighter than it normally would have been since somebody had broken into the house night before last, stealing the best sarongs and trousers in the cabinet, along with her new *kabaya* from Jakarta. She had saved for weeks to buy that blouse with its lace fringes and had planned to wear it to Wadi's wedding that Saturday. Mother had talked about calling the police, but Father had said, "What's the use? The police are the most corrupt people in the village. They were probably behind it anyway." With half the clothes in the house gone, there wasn't all that much to wash today and so much the better, since she was tired of doing the laundry. The work was too hard and she always ended up breaking a fingernail and chipping the bright red polish she had so painstakingly applied to her fingers the night before. Why did she always have to do this donkeywork? She hated it. She knew that Father could afford to hire a girl from the neighboring village, where they were so poor they ate brown rice, dirty and unpolished, like animals. If only Father would hire somebody, then she, Dik Dik, could follow her dream to work in Ning Ning's beauty salon.

Tuesdays were the low point of the week as far as Dik Dik was concerned. After morning prayers at the mosque, she had to come back to the house, gather firewood, light a fire in the stove and cook breakfast for the whole family. Just fanning the fire to get it started took a long time; sometimes, the sparks flew and once, they started a fire when they landed in a bunch of old rags near the woodpile. Then she had to dress her three nieces for school, pressing the little blue-and-white uniforms with an iron heated over the fire. After they were clothed and combed, she stood with the three little girls until Udin came along on his motorcycle to collect them for the two-mile drive to the schoolhouse, balancing two of them in front of him between the handlebars while the third clung to his waist from behind. Dik Dik hated standing out in the road like that, not looking her best. No make-up on and hair a mess, not to mention clothes that looked like they had been slept in which, she had to admit, was often the case. But what was the point of getting dressed up and looking nice when she had to lug the laundry down to the river and spend two hours getting splashed with soapy water and bleach? And put up with those other women and their silly tongues, running on about everything and nothing? Who cares if Suni's son is going to be circumcised next month? What does it matter if somebody stole a mat from the women's section of the mosque or that Yayat can't afford to buy a ticket for the *haj* trip? The only stories she liked were the spicy ones, but you seldom heard that kind of tale in a strait-laced village like this one. Well, sometimes you did, especially if Sri were around. You could always count on Sri to liven things up. There was that story Sri told about the young mullah and his wife. Dik Dik loved hearing it. It gave her goose bumps just thinking about the details. The mullah was handsome and looked like Omar Sharif and had that, well, you know, that BIG bulge in his trousers that looked like he was carrying a bunch of bananas between his legs.

How the women laughed when Sri got into her stories. Well, about this handsome mullah, Sri said that once, during Ramadan, she felt sorry for him having to get up so early before the call to prayer and she worried about his not having breakfast, so she decided to surprise him and his wife with a treat. The night before, she fixed a special dish of coconut rice and next morning, while it was still dark, she walked to the mullah's house with her basket. When she got to the house, it was still quiet and dark so she decided to go round the back to the kitchen and just drop off her treat. Maybe she would never even tell him where it came from. At the kitchen door, she heard some noise coming from inside, nothing loud, just some shuffling and what sounded like a whisper. She knew that she should probably knock or call out, but somehow curiosity got the best of her so she just pushed the door open. And there was the mullah, completely nude! He was standing there, yes, standing there, and he and his wife were DOING IT, yes, DOING IT, before her very eyes. Imagine! In the kitchen! And his "you know what," well, that was even bigger than we thought it would be! Imagine! In the kitchen! And standing! Sri was so shocked she just froze and couldn't move. And the mullah and his wife, they just stood there too, in that same position!

The shame of it! Then Sri felt her heart fluttering and pounding and before she knew it, she had dropped her basket, spilling the rice pudding all over the mullah's kitchen floor. When she stooped to clean up the mess, she got dizzy and felt herself falling. As she keeled over in his direction, her face went right into the mullah's crotch and her nose hit his . . . THING! That BIG AWFUL THING! Whenever Sri told this story, she had to pause at this point, catch her breath and fan herself rapidly with both hands. Well, you can imagine Sri's dilemma.

How could she ever show her face in that mosque again? Every time she would pray, she could only think of one thing! And it drove her crazy. Well, you know what Sri ended up doing? She converted and became a Catholic. Yes, a Catholic in a Muslim village! She had to travel ten miles, all the way to Tasik to go to the church, but what a relief. And you know, not long after she converted and became a Catholic, Sri experienced a miracle. When she joined the Catholics, they had told her about miracles, but she never dreamed it could happen to her. Well, it did. Every time she prayed at Saint Mary's in Tasik, she looked up at the statue of Jesus and saw that handsome mullah's face looking down on her. His big round eyes and those full lips were smiling down, just like the time when she was scooping up the rice from his kitchen floor. Oh my goodness! The incense and the music brought it all back and she almost swooned every time she went to church. It was better than going to those double-feature Indian films where the beautiful lady gets kidnapped and then rescued by the handsome hero. Oh my! Her palms got sweaty and the prayer beads got damp and she went kind of light-headed and knew it was a miracle. That Sri was so bad!

Dik Dik reached the top the hill and lifted the load of laundry from her head. She thought about the mullah and his wife. Why were they doing it in the kitchen? That kind of thing is supposed to be done in the bedroom, lying down. She couldn't understand them standing in the kitchen. She would have to ask Ning Ning about it. Ning Ning knew a lot about that kind of thing. Setting out again with the pan hoisted on her head, arms lifted up for support and hips swaying slightly as she moved along the road, she was a pretty sight even though her clothes were old and there were splashes of water on her sarong. She passed a bunch of high school boys on their way to class; handsome rascals in their grey trousers and white shirts with their book bags slung rakishly over their shoulders. Some had short hair, others wore it longer, slicked up with gel and spiked out. One of them whistled at her and she tossed her head and pouted in mock disapproval.

If only she had been wearing something nice and had her face done right, she'd have the whole crowd of them in the palm of her hand. But why was she thinking about these boys, just kids, when she was so much older, already twenty-two? When she got back to the house, it was quiet. Her parents had already left for the furniture factory. Father worked on the assembly line with a lathe, making legs for stools and tables and Mother served tea to the workers and kept the bathrooms clean. Time to relax for a minute before going to the market. Time to put on some make-up and change into decent street clothes.

Dik Dik stood before the mirror. Her figure was petite and small waisted, hips narrow with legs well shaped. Her face was longish and beautifully pale, not dark like most of the village girls, who looked like buffaloes. She had eyes that were set off by arched brows and a beauty mark just below her right cheekbone. Her nose was slender and led to full lips that curled up at the edges. Below her dimpled chin was a slender, swanlike throat from which protruded a rather prominent Adam's apple. She touched the Adam's apple, wishing it were not there.

That bump on her throat was the only outward sign that Dik Dik was not all girl. In fact, she was a man. Or at least that's what her parents had told her even though she felt and acted like a woman and did everything she could to be one. There was one big problem that really developed into a nuisance when Dik Dik became a teenager. It was her penis, which was a very large one. She measured it once when it was erect and it was nearly ten inches long! When she was fourteen, it started acting up in a most disagreeable and unladylike way. But clever girl that she was, she figured out a way to deal with this thing that she really considered not a part of her. One day, when she was visiting the furniture factory, she sneaked a roll of duct tape out of the shipping department. With a strip of the duct tape firmly in place under her panties, she scarcely noticed her manhood. And when it got aroused or unruly, she just sat down, crossed her legs and squeezed it to death. She had gone to a *dukun* (witch doctor) to see if it could be removed or made to disappear, but so far, the potions hadn't produced the desired result. Anyway, with the duct tape, she had it pretty much under control.

What she really wanted was a little more upstairs. She had learned how to use the duct tape – that tape was SO useful – to compress her nonexistent breasts into a ripple of flesh, producing a lovely cleavage that showed to great advantage when she wore her low-cut blouses. If the *dukun* could help her a little in that department, that was all she needed. When she managed to scrape together a few rupiahs, she would go back to the *dukun* with her new request. And if all else failed, there were falsies; even some of the other real women used them to make up for what nature had forgot. She had felt female ever since she was born and by now, her parents and the whole village were used to the fact that she looked and acted like a girl. In fact, she was quite popular with the village boys and men and some of the girls who used to be her friends in school were now jealous of all the attention she got. She always got special treatment at the market from the man who sold fish. He would put an extra one on the scale after charging her and then give her arm a little squeeze and lick his lips as he slipped the wiggling creatures into a plastic bag. He even invited her to go fishing with him, but she never dared accept his offer, even though she wanted to.

One evening, when she had been helping Ning Ning in the beauty salon, a man she had never seen before came into the shop. It was late and nearly closing time. Ning Ning had left early and told Dik Dik to lock the door and leave after she had cleaned up. She had noticed this man standing out on the street, smoking a cigarette. He had been there for a long time before he walked over and entered the salon. For a minute, he stood silently at the door, watching her move around while she swept up the hair that had collected on the floor. He was still young, not more than thirty, and had a full mustache and rather wild, curly, jet-black hair. He said he wanted to buy some lipstick for his sister and wanted Dik Dik's advice about what he should get. Dik Dik was flattered that somebody would consult her on such an important matter and set about showing him the different types of cosmetics in the shop. They chatted away and she found herself enjoying the visitor and the interest he showed in her and her expertise. On impulse, she darted to the back of the shop, to the storeroom where Ning Ning kept the items she reserved for special customers, the Shiseido Rainbow Selection and the very rare products from

America by Avon. As she stooped over to retrieve these treasures, she felt the man come up behind her, pushing the front of his body into her backside. She wiggled and twitched in response and before she knew it, they were locked in an embrace, just like she had seen in those Hindi movies. They stayed in the backroom a long time and Dik Dik began to worry that her mother might come looking for her. After a particularly tight hug and a long kiss in what he told her was the French style, she broke away from him when she heard the evening call to prayer, saying that she had to meet her parents at the mosque. As she hurried out the door, the man gave her a final squeeze and said that he would be back again, whispering his name as he disappeared into the darkness. Hadi is what she thought she heard him say.

Hadi became a regular visitor to the salon. He never did buy anything and Dik Dik began to think his question about the lipstick was a trick. But it didn't matter. Hadi was nice to her and made her feel like a real woman. Sometimes, he even brought her little presents. One time, it was a pink plastic tote bag with a pokemon design, not the real thing, but a nice enough knock-off; on another occasion he appeared with a T-shirt with "You Send Me" written on it. Hadi said that was English, but he hadn't a clue about what it meant. Their routine was always the same. He would hang out in the street till Ning Ning left the shop; then he would come in the door and they would head right to the backroom, skipping the preliminaries and polite conversation.

Hadi taught Dik Dik quite a few things. He called them games and gave each one of them names. There was "Lend a Helping Hand," which was easy and quick. They did that one when Hadi was in a hurry or when Dik Dik wasn't in the mood for much else. Then there was Dik Dik's favorite, which they called "Playing the Flute." That took longer and sometimes, Hadi wanted to wait after they had finished and have Dik Dik play the flute a second time. Between sets, Dik Dik would take out a pack of cards and play solitaire while Hadi smoked a *kretek* (clove) cigarette, waiting for the flute to come back again. On special occasions, they would indulge in Hadi's favorite game, which he called "Riding Down the Hershey Highway." At first it hurt a lot, but then Dik Dik got used to it and Hadi said it was much better than a real woman. That made Dik Dik really proud to think that she could beat real women at their own game.

Life went on like that for quite sometime. Hadi never talked very much, but he was nice and always told Dik Dik how pretty she was. Dik Dik got a little embarrassed about all those gifts and wondered how she could explain where they came from to her parents. And where DID all those nice things come from? Although Hadi was neat and clean, he wore plain clothes and looked kind of poor. Didn't have a car or a motorcycle, or even a bike, for that matter. So how could he afford so many presents? She had put them in a trunk in her bedroom, but now the trunk was almost full. His latest present was really something special, a Sony CD player, wafer-thin, with delicate earphones that felt like earrings when she put them on. The only problem was there was no sound when she turned the player on. Hadi said that he would try to get it repaired, but even without the sound, it didn't matter. Dik Dik enjoyed just looking in the little window, tapping her foot to an imaginary tune and watching the silvery CD spin around. Hadi usually came to the salon on Tuesdays and Saturdays. But then, he stopped coming. One week, two weeks, then a month. No Hadi. Dik Dik was beside herself, wondering what had happened. Was he bored with Dik Dik? Had he found another woman? Did he move away, going back to where he came from? After all, he wasn't from West Java; maybe he went back to Sumatra.

Dik Dik seemed to remember he had said he was from Sumatra, but she wasn't sure. All she knew was that his accent was different and that he didn't speak Sundanese, the local language.

Dik Dik grew depressed and desperate. The longer Hadi stayed away, the more she realized that she was really stuck on him. One day, she broke down and confided to Ning Ning, telling her everything. She was surprised when Ning Ning told her that she knew the whole story already. When people are wildly infatuated, they reveal far more than they realize and Dik Dik's dilemma was plain enough, Ning Ning said. She had lost her man and now they had to find a way to get him back. Men are all louses; as soon as they have you in their power, they drop you and look for something new. We'll just have to fix that and make it worth his while to come back to you. Some of her clients had seen Hadi in the big bazaar in Tasik. He wasn't shopping or selling anything; just standing around watching people as they came and went. Kind of strange, don't you think? Anyway, he was still around and when the time was right, Ning Ning said, she knew how to get him and bring him back to his senses, and to Dik Dik.

Dik Dik was too forlorn to speculate about what he had been doing in the bazaar, but perked up quickly when Ning Ning laid out her plan. Ning Ning explained as delicately as she could that, as beautiful as she was, Dik Dik lacked one special thing to make her a real woman. She didn't have a *nonok*, a woman's special spot, and they had to get one for her. Then when Hadi came back to her, she could keep him forever. It sounded like a good plan, but Dik Dik was a little puzzled about how she could get that special spot and have her own personal *nonok*. She said that she had been to the *dukun*, had paid her a lot of money for the *jamu* (potions), but she never got what had been promised. Ning Ning dismissed the tale about the *dukun* and said "Leave it to me. I know somebody who goes to Hong Kong on business trips and he can bring back what you need. It won't be cheap, but you can work off the cost by coming to the salon every evening and cleaning the place instead of fooling around in the backroom all night, like I know you've been doing!" Dik Dik said she would do anything in the world to get her own *nonok* and went home full of hope.

Dik Dik could think of nothing else. Night and day, it was *nonok* that was on her mind. She got through her chores and didn't even hear the tedious tattling of the women down at the river when she did her weekly wash. She would launder her mother's batiks and her father's sarongs, lay them on the rocks to dry in the sun and just look out in space at the distant rice fields and rows of tea growing up in the hills and think about what was coming soon from Hong Kong. She even stopped using the duct tape down below and up above, knowing that when she had her *nonok*, nothing could stop her. Days and days passed, but nothing happened. Time began to pass so slowly. Every evening, she would stop by the salon and ask Ning Ning if it had arrived. Ning Ning seemed so preoccupied these days and would scarcely take the time to answer her. Maybe it was all a cruel joke and she was being made fun of, like when she was in grade school and all the other kids used to pick on her for being a boy who acted like a girl. "You're just a stupid *banchi* (drag queen), Dik Dik!" She could still hear their nasty little voices and her ears got red with shame when she thought of it. But then, she showed everybody. She grew up beautiful, prettier than the real girls in her class, who were now old and fat, with a baby hanging off of each hip. And she had never been mean to anybody in spite of the insults and cruelty they had thrown at her. She had even stayed up all night, stitching a wedding gown for the biggest tormentor in her class. That seemed to turn people around and Dik Dik came to be accepted as one of the village women.

One morning, when she was depressed and had practically given up hope of ever seeing her *nonok*, Ning Ning's younger sister came racing into the kitchen as Dik Dik was preparing breakfast. "Come over to the salon right away," she said. After breakfast, she told her mother that she was not feeling well and had to go to the village clinic. Of course, that was not her real destination. When she arrived at the salon, Ning Ning pushed a package into her hands. She opened the sky-blue box and under layers of gauzy tissue, there it was. Pink, like the skin of European women, squishy and soft in the right places, but firm where it should be firm, there was Dik Dik's own personal *nonok*. She removed it from the box and put it up to her face, rubbing it against her cheek. It felt so real. When she held it up, she realized that it looked like a bikini she had seen on a page ripped out of one of those naughty magazines her uncle had brought back from Australia. She took it into the backroom and tried it on for size. The little elasticized straps held firmly against her legs and it fit like a charm. The only problem was her own real "thing" kept getting in the way. Well, she could take care of that pretty quickly with a good, tight application of duct tape.

That would teach the useless botheration to rear its head again when it was not wanted!

She looked in the mirror, turning left and right, and decided right there and then to give her *nonok* its own name. She called it Suzy. Her own little Suzy. The only thing was that Suzy was pink and Dik Dik was brown. What to do? She removed Suzy and inspected her under the light. As she did so, she detected an odor that she had not noticed before in her excitement. Suzy had a distinctly industrial odor, like those cheap plastic sandals they used to get from Communist China back in the old days when Sukarno ran the country. She must talk to Ning Ning about this before they settled on a price and how Dik Dik could work it off. When she returned to the front of the salon, Ning Ning dismissed her questions with a wave of the hand and a shake of her head. So what if you're a different color? In the dark, who's going to see? And if you're so concerned, I'll give you some of that Shiseido to smear on your tummy and you'll be pink all over. And don't worry about that smell. Just light up a *kretek* (clove) cigarette when you undress and nobody will know the difference. And if you doubt me, I'll give you some Midnight in Shanghai feminine deodorant. You can spray that around your spot and plastic will be the last thing that will come to mind! Why are you so silly? You should thank me for all the trouble I went to for you! Dik Dik felt grateful and ashamed as she left the salon after promising to work every night for a month to pay for her Suzy.

Days and weeks passed with no sign of Hadi. At first, Dik Dik thought of asking Ning Ning's help again. She had told Dik Dik that Hadi had been seen in Tasik. Maybe Ning Ning knew more than she was telling. But now, it didn't seem to matter anymore whether he came to see her or not. Since she got her Suzy, Dik Dik was so happy she didn't seem to need anybody or anything. At last she felt like a real woman. Of course, she still had to use duct tape. On some days, when that funny feeling came on strong, she had to use a double tape to keep Mr. You-Know-What in place. But Suzy was on top, so to speak, and when Dik Dik looked in the long mirror at the back of the salon, she was happy because what you see is what you get, and she saw Suzy, pink and beautiful, down there where she should be.

There were some small things that worried Dik Dik from time to time. One was the rumor that the furniture factory was going broke because business was bad. Father said he had even heard whispers coming from the owner's office that they might have to declare bankruptcy and go out of business. When she thought about that, Dik Dik went into a panic. If there was no factory, her supply of duct tape would dry up. Where could she find it otherwise? From the box it came in, she knew that it was foreign. She knew that "Made in USA" meant foreign. Somewhere far away; at least as far as Hong Kong or Singapore. If the factory closed, she would be done for. Without the duct tape, "Thingumajig" would keep acting up and maybe even damage Suzy! Sometimes, when that feeling got really strong, Dik Dik could feel the pressure on poor little Suzy. One of these days, she might even break.

Right then and there, Dik Dik made two important decisions. First, she would stop wearing Suzy at night when she went to bed. She loved Suzy and felt that she was a part of Dik Dik, but you have to do what you have to do and she knew that at this point, Suzy needed a rest. The second decision involved some planning and would not be as easy. It involved getting what amounted to a lifetime supply of duct tape from the factory before it closed down and left her in the lurch. She had to develop a plan. It wasn't easy getting into the supply room. In fact, it was especially difficult to get to that area where all of the imported goods were kept. They couldn't be paid for with rupiah and had to be bought with dollars, which were very scarce and expensive, she had heard. There was always a clerk or a guard at the door to the special storeroom. The only way she had managed to get the duct tape before was to wait till the coast was clear and nobody was there. That was when the guard had to go to the bathroom or walk out for a cup of tea. She had gone in and slipped one or two rolls into her purse and was able to make tracks before anybody saw her. Now she needed BOXES of tape!

The plan Dik Dik developed was simple but brilliant and involved those two friends of the desperate, bribery and charm. She had noticed the security guard before. He was young and nice-looking and Mother said that he was single. He came from that poor village over the hill. People were so poor and backward there that they didn't even have television yet. Imagine! He was the answer to her duct tape problem. She began to visit the factory more often, stopping by the supply room door to say hello and chat with the guard. His name was Bang Bang. She increased her charm offensive and started bringing Bang Bang tea and cakes every afternoon. He was talkative and lonely and was really rather a nice hayseed.

One day, she upped the stakes and brought Bang Bang a present, saying she knew his birthday was coming soon.

She really had no idea when it was, but she figured sooner or later, everybody has to have a birthday. And she had that whole trunk full of presents from Hadi that were at home, just gathering dust. She selected one of the last things Hadi had given her. Bang Bang was flattered and excited when she gave it to him. It was a baseball cap with "You're a Bad Motherfucker" written on the front. They both agreed it was beautiful and that what was written was certainly foreign. Dik Dik giggled and said it was probably something romantic. Bang Bang began to look at Dik Dik in a different way. Before, it was all friendly joking and chitchat. Since the birthday present, he would gaze at her with cow eyes, sometimes staring out into space as though he were lost in thought. Dik Dik asked him what was the matter and Bang Bang would reply, "Oh, nothing." When she told her about it, Ning Ning snorted and said, "The fool's in love with you!"

Dik Dik felt the time had now come to act on her plan. She knew it had when Bang Bang told her that afternoon that he had a new job. At first, she almost died of shock, thinking her whole plan had been destroyed, but then she could scarcely believe her ears when she heard Bang Bang say that he had been moved to the night shift! Dik Dik knew that she was within reach of an endless supply of duct tape and that it was time to bring Suzy into action. Bang Bang's new shift was 6:00 P.M. to 6:00 A.M. After dinner and prayers at the mosque, Dik Dik arrived at the factory. She was wearing a man's raincoat and had a big hat on her head. It hung down over her face and she hoped nobody could see who she was. This time, she was not walking, but driving a *becak* (rickshaw). In the dark, no one would know that she was not a *becak* driver.

What a clever plan this was! It had occurred to her earlier that day, when she was down at the river with those silly cows doing the laundry. They asked her why she was so quiet and she hadn't answered, she was so deep in thought. She knew from riding in *becaks* that they were wide enough to hold at least two big boxes of duct tape. Her uncle was a *becak* driver and always parked the *becak* in their back-yard when he stopped pedaling, usually at about four in the afternoon. It was perfect! Dik Dik brought the *becak* to a halt and parked it in a small shed, out of sight. It wouldn't do if the *becak* were stolen while she was in the supply room with Bang Bang.

She had thought of everything. She might be a girl, but she wasn't dizzy-headed like those other silly gooses in her class. For the first time in her life, she was glad that she was a man, or at least that she had the good judgment of one. She had also brought a pack of *kretek* cigarettes. She knew Bang Bang liked them and that lighting one would prevent Suzy from smelling like an old rubber san-dal. Just to be on the safe side, she had liberally sprayed her "spot" with Midnight in Shanghai. It was so strong that it made her sneeze. Bang Bang was there, sitting in his chair about to doze off. He had not gotten used to the night shift yet and by 9:00 P.M. was usually in bed. It was approaching 10:00 P.M. now and it was hard for him to fight off slumber. Dik Dik was secretly delighted when she saw him in this somniferous state. She offered him a *kretek* and they both lit up. Suzy was safe behind the clouds of clove smoke.

Dik Dik's mind raced forward in a way she had never experienced before. Counting backwards, she knew she had to be out of the factory within an hour, or an hour and a half at the latest. It would take her half an hour to pedal back home in the *becak*. If she reached home after midnight, there was the risk that Father might see her when she came in with the boxes. Before that time, he always slept like a log, but after twelve, he usually got up to pee nearly every hour. She didn't want to think about peeing just now or any other time. It was always inconvenient and sometimes painful when she got the call of nature. Stripping the duct tape off was no picnic. In fact, it hurt like hell. That's why Dik Dik stopped drinking water or any other liquid, for that matter. Mother noticed it and told her that if she didn't drink lots of water and hot tea, she would get constipated. Dik Dik nodded in agreement, but decided she would rather be constipated than have to remove that duct tape. Ouch! It was painful just thinking about it!

Dik Dik and Suzy now moved into high gear. Bang Bang was still sleepy and a bit silly, which suited Dik Dik's purposes. They joked for a minute and then leading him by the hand, she pulled him into the back room, saying she wanted to show him something. Getting him out of his chair was no problem because Dik Dik was strong and Bang Bang was even shorter than she was. Once her eyes got accustomed to the dark, Dik Dik spotted the prized boxes. Luckily they were on top of the pile of supplies. So much the better for a quick lift and a speedy getaway. Dik Dik recalled those evenings in the back of the salon and began to play Hadi's games with Bang Bang. First, she lent him a helping hand and then when the flute got ready to play, she blew out a little melody. She wondered as she was performing why they used the word "blow." Blowing had nothing to do with it, although it could be

kind of nice for the cooling-off period. Dik Dik decided
to skip "Riding the Hershey Highway." Why did she need
the highway when she had Suzy? Enough of somebody
else's games! She wanted to invent her own. And so she
started "Wake Up Ya Little Suzy." Midnight in Shanghai
was still going strong and the game was a great success.

But trouble was brewing down below. Thingumabob
was causing trouble under the duct tape and Dik Dik felt
the adhesive starting to give way. Luckily, at that moment,
Bang Bang collapsed on the floor in a happy pile of sleep.
Just in time. There was a ripping sound as the duct tape
loosened and Suzy flew off and dropped on the floor,
landing on Bang Bang's snoring face. Dik Dik stooped
over Bang Bang, snatched Suzy from Bang Bang's nose
and stuffed her into the raincoat's pocket. Then with more
strength than she knew she had, Dik Dik lifted the two
boxes of duct tape and staggered under their weight to
the shed, where the *becak* was waiting. She pedaled home
in the misty darkness without seeing a soul. It must have
been past midnight.

Dik Dik slept late the following morning. It wasn't till
she heard Father shuffling about that she realized there
was a fire to light and breakfast to cook. Then there was
the cursed laundry to do down by the river. She had managed to slip into the house the night before without wak-
ing anybody. The two boxes were safe in her room, in the
corner under a stack of mats and long pieces of cloth that
had been bought for curtains that never got made. Nobody would notice that the pile was a couple of feet
higher. Mother and Father hardly ever set foot in the room
anyway.

Everything had gone according to plan, without the

slightest slip-up. But Dik Dik was still worried. What if the factory manager discovered that two boxes of duct tape were missing? Surely he would. It was only a matter of time before they would need some more and when they came looking for it, they would end up pointing the finger at poor Bang Bang. And then it would be all over. At least for him. He would probably lose his job and maybe even go to jail. Her thoughts were interrupted by Mother asking where breakfast was. Later in the morning, when the girls had been packed off to school and her parents had left for the factory, Dik Dik reached in the pocket of the raincoat and extracted Suzy. Looking limp and used, Suzy reeked of Midnight in Shanghai gone sour, with the stench of old urine. Dik Dik usually washed Suzy once a week and it was high time that she had her bath. Dik Dik would take care of that shortly down by the river. She would give Suzy a good scrubbing along with the sarongs and other laundry, then set her out on a rock to dry in the sun. In the meantime, she needed to do some repairs on Suzy. One of the straps had been ripped last night. Was it during the game or just afterwards, when that stupid Thingumajig acted up? Whatever. A little stitching would fix everything and Suzy would be right as rain.

Dik Dik lifted the load and settled it on her head for the long walk down to the river. Suzy had been repaired and now, her thoughts turned once again to the plight of Bang Bang. She would have to tell him before it was too late that if ever anybody questioned him about the missing boxes, he would have to deny all responsibility, saying that he had been at his post all night and had seen nothing. How could they prove him wrong? Well, that was his problem. When it came to duct tape and saving Suzy, Bang Bang just had to take a back seat and suffer the consequences. In any case, she decided not to confide in him about her little caper. It would be too difficult to explain herself out of that one. Besides, what he didn't know wouldn't hurt him.

Dik Dik arrived at the riverbank and was glad to see that almost nobody was there. She had thought about going off by herself to a remote spot and doing her wash out of sight of the others, but that just wouldn't do. There would be talk about why she was behaving so strangely. She knew that she'd better watch her Ps and Qs since her being accepted as a woman hadn't been all that easy, and now that she really was one, with Suzy's help, she didn't want to blot her copy book. She settled on her usual rock and began the laundry, doing the batiks first. Suzy could come later, when the crowd had thinned out. No-

body except Ning Ning knew about Suzy and she wanted to keep it that way.

After a while, she was joined by her neighbor, Itjeh and Itjeh's cat, Kuning. Kuning was a huge, gray tomcat who followed Itjeh everywhere she went, more like a dog than a cat. For some reason, Kuning loved Dik Dik even though she didn't have any time for cats. He was always coming up and rubbing himself against Dik Dik's legs. Dik Dik couldn't stand it and wanted to kick the cat, but didn't dare to in front of Itjeh. As the two girls washed and chatted, Kuning circled about the rock, purring loudly. Usually he fell asleep in the sun, but today, he was strangely active. Then Dik Dik saw why. Kuning had noticed Suzy on the rock a few feet from the girls. He lifted his nose in the air and bobbed his head, appreciatively catching the stale scent of Shanghai pee. It seemed to drive him crazy and he raced to Suzy, nuzzling her and taking deep sniffs.

Then he began a game that involved pawing Suzy, pushing her farther down the rock away from Dik Dik. In horror, Dik Dik watched from the corner of her eye, not wanting to reveal her anxiety to Itjeh. That damned cat! How she longed to stand up, take a soaking wet sarong and knock the crap out of that feline howler. What good was he? Not even a mouser! Itjeh's house was full of rats because they spoiled Kuning and fed him like he was a member of the family. And now, this! Dik Dik wanted to jump up and down and scream bloody murder, but she was frozen, with Itjeh yammering on like a magpie. Suddenly, Kuning grabbed Suzy in his jaws and scampered off the rock, running in the direction of the other women down closer to the river. Losing her wits in a mad frenzy, Dik Dik bolted up and ran after the cat. He had stopped for a minute and was aggressively chewing the soft pink plastic that was Suzy's heart and soul. Now just inches behind the cat, Dik Dik lunged to grab Suzy, but the wily Kuning had scampered away as Dik Dik fell on her face on the rocks. Again, Kuning paused and looked back at Dik Dik. He was enjoying this game that she was playing with him. By this time, the other women noticed what had become a commotion and stopped to watch the chase. Dik Dik looked plaintively at them, half explaining and half crying, "The cat's stolen Suzy. The cat's got my *nonok*, my vagina!" By now, Kuning, in a fit of fun, had scampered up the hill, out of sight. Dik Dik, out of breath and chafing with skinned elbows and embarrassment, collapsed on a rock, murmuring, "The cat stole my *nonok*, the cat stole my Suzy!" The other women burst into gales of giggles, shouting, "Dik Dik, you don't HAVE a vagina! You're a drag queen! Did you forget that?" Dik Dik lunged at the nearest woman, grabbing her by the shoulders, shaking her violently till her teeth rattled like a dozen pair of castanets. "Tell that to your husband the next time he comes home late, you wrinkled trashcan! And ask him where's he's been and who's better, Dik Dik or you?" The group grew so quiet you could have heard a rat piss on cotton.

Dik Dik gathered her half-done laundry, slapped it into the aluminum pan and marched up the hill. If Mother complained about the clothes not being washed, she'd tell her to do them herself! Back home, she sat on the kitchen floor, not knowing which way to turn. Bang Bang would probably be in jail. The village women had disowned her and most important, the cat had dragged Suzy off and had probably chewed her to death. She was about to go out of her mind when suddenly, Thingumabob began to act up. It must have been all that blood racing around her body. Normally, he didn't show his fangs till later in the day. Well, at least it took her mind off of the morning's tragedies. When her head began to clear, all Dik Dik could think of was revenge. She MUST poison that cat. Of course Itjeh would suspect her, but let her prove it.

Dik Dik had to get out of the house. She decided to go down to the mosque and say a few prayers, one for Suzy and another for Bang Bang. She changed her wet sarong and washed her face. A little make-up made her feel better and by the time she got to the mosque, her mood was lifting. It lifted even higher when she looked up and saw the handsome mullah up on the roof of the mosque. What a queer place for him to be! He was squatting up there and the wind had blown his sarong up so that his handsome legs were gleaming in the sun. When Dik Dik got closer, she saw the mullah was petting a cat. It was Kuning and he still had Suzy in his jaws. He was rolling on his back while the mullah scratched his head. Dik Dik raced up to the edge of the mosque and waved at the mullah. He waved back and called down to her, laughing, "I don't know what the cat has found. What is this funny thing?" Dik Dik shouted back, "It's mine. Something I need. Will you please bring it down to me?" The mullah plucked Suzy from the cat's mouth and held her for a moment between with his thumb and forefinger before descending the shaky bamboo ladder, dropping to the ground in front of Dik Dik. Suzy had a few tooth marks here and there, but was not much worse for wear. As the mullah handed her back to Dik Dik in what she thought was a rather ceremonious manner, he winked and said, "Don't forget to come to evening prayers tonight, I'll be waiting for you!"

CHAPTER NINE
SAM OGLESBY, COUNTRY DOCTOR

Devoted to the Poor, He Died in Poverty

Doctor Samuel Cecil Oglesby was thoroughly Virginian even though he spent his years of medical school in the "foreign" state of Maryland, at Johns Hopkins University in Baltimore. Oglesby was born into a large family of Southwest Virginia rural gentry near Wytheville in the early 1870s. Among his numerous siblings, he counted three brothers who were medical doctors. Perhaps, this led him to go into "doctoring," as his homespun Tangier wife dubbed the profession. He was raised by a stern mother, Mary Francis Oglesby, who was remembered by later generations of the family for refusing to buy his brother out of the Army after he impetuously enlisted as a volunteer in the Spanish-American War. After completing an undergraduate degree at William and Mary in Williamsburg, Virginia, he excelled in medical school and was first in his class, specializing in Gynecology. "I know my women," he used to say in his thick Virginia drawl. But these academic achievements did not launch him on a brilliant career. He began his working life as a railroad physician, riding trains in Virginia and into Baltimore. Soon he abandoned the rails and his bachelorhood for Tangier Island, Virginia, where he settled down as the island's first doctor, marrying a waterman's daughter named Nona Virginia Crockett Parks. She was a young widow who had been married only a short time to an oysterman who died after overexposure in a winter storm on the Chesapeake Bay.

How and why Doctor Oglesby found himself practicing medicine on tiny, isolated Tangier is not clear. But it seems that religion played a part. Sometime after graduating from medical school, family lore has it that he "received the word" and began preaching. Whether his revivalist itinerary landed him in Tangier by chance or by intention is not clear. Perhaps he was drawn to the island, since it had become somewhat of a meeting place for the seriously faithful.

The Oglesby family remained on Tangier for some years, probably less than ten. Their only child, a son named Samuel Crockett Oglesby, was born on Tangier in October 1911. His birth was premature and the severe winter brought anxiety to his parents when long periods of freeze iced the Chesapeake Bay and isolated Tangier, preventing shipments of food and other essentials from being delivered to the islanders. According to his mother, young Samuel's main source of nourishment that first, hard winter was saltine crackers and milk. An earlier child, a daughter, had died in childbirth, and the Oglesbys decided their son's chances of survival were better on the mainland.

They resettled in a village called Girdletree in Worcester County, on the Eastern Shore of Maryland. Once again, the reasons Doctor Oglesby and his family were drawn to this one-horse town are unclear. Neither side of the family – Oglesby or Crockett – had relatives or friends in the area. Professional considerations probably led them to choose the spot since no doctors were practicing near there at the time

Dr. Oglesby soon became well loved for his medical expertise and his way with people. He was given to anecdotes and folksy parables, which endeared him to the locals. An old lady reminisced some sixty years after the fact about having her tonsils removed as a child by Dr. Oglesby. When she asked him if she could eat some ice cream her mother had made for the family, he replied, "I want you to want it, but you can't have it just yet."

By all accounts, the Oglesbys had a simple, hardworking and rather threadbare existence. Exotic food items like bananas were seldom available in those days on the Eastern Shore, and the carcass of a coconut brought long ago from Florida was on display in the front parlor, a symbol of distant, never-experienced pleasures. Mrs. Oglesby, or Miz Nonie to her friends and family, was a frugal, spare-the-frills homemaker. Nothing – but nothing – was wasted or thrown away in her household. Ashes from the wood stove and excess grease from the kitchen were saved for making soap; even waste from the "slop jar" – there being no indoor plumbing then – was spread on rose bushes that climbed the outhouse and barn and bloomed gloriously in summer. Empty feed sacks bearing the imprinted likeness of pigs, cows and chickens were washed, cut and stitched into undergarments and nightshirts. Laughter could be heard in the darkness upstairs when a kerosene lamp-bearing wearer of a pig-emblazoned nightshirt was encountered in the hallway.

His patients were anything but affluent and the doctor's seeming lack of concern about money matters and his willingness to treat patients who couldn't pay left the Oglesby family at little more than a subsistence level. Their genteel poverty did not affect them in the early years since their son's two-room schoolhouse was within walking distance of home, and a kitchen garden and hen house provided most of their table needs. In those days, rural Maryland was mostly a barter economy, and patients, more often than not, paid their medical bills in kind with farm produce and preserved goods. Only later in their lives did the Oglesbys realize the support a nest egg could have provided. Nona Oglesby became a practical nurse and assisted her doc-

tor-husband when patients came to call. She always
addressed him as "Doctor," never calling her husband
by his given name, even in private conversations. Highly
intelligent and likeable, she felt at ease at any level of
society and was one of those people for whom lack of a
formal education was no hindrance. They operated as
a team and received the medical practice at home,
where an office had been created. In the afternoon,
Dr. Oglesby set out on his rounds in the countryside,
making house calls, riding in a horse-drawn buggy, often accompanied by his son whose one wish was to become a doctor like his father.

Dr. Oglesby was addicted to baseball. He later developed another addiction, which was to be his undo-
ing. One afternoon, coming back later than usual from
his calls on rural patients, he parked the buggy in its
customary place. The horse, hungry and impatient to
be fed, bolted just as its harness was being detached.
The doctor was alighting from the carriage at that very
minute and was thrown to the ground, falling on a pile
of sand. It was a short and seemingly gentle fall, but he
broke his hip. The fracture was complicated. Medical
technology of the time – the early 1920s – had not advanced sufficiently to deal successfully with such frac-
tures, so the doctor's remaining years were filled with
pain. At a certain point, he began administering pain-
killers to himself and came to rely on morphine to ease
the discomfort. He continued to practice medicine,
but demons increasingly invaded his life. He died from
a bout of pneumonia in 1923. His passing was also the
beginning of the end of a noble institution, the country physician. Doctors no longer devote their lives to

country life, with its hard work and little monetary compensation. Places like Tangier Island, Virginia and Girdletree, Maryland haven't seen a doctor in generations.

The postscript to his life, the fate of his wife and twelve-year-old son, is a story of misfortune being overcome by strength of character and resilience. Impoverished, with no family to turn to, the two of them managed to survive and even to send Dr. Oglesby's son, Sam, to college at the University of Maryland. His outstanding scholarship won him admission to medical school, but the dream of becoming a doctor eluded him for lack of money. A plea for help to the well-heeled Oglesby family in Southwest Virginia resulted in the gift of a Bible. They had never been happy about Dr. Oglesby's marriage to a simple waterman's daughter and they displayed their displeasure accordingly.

Sam Oglesby had several careers, but he never ceased to be interested in the science of medicine, which he studied as a hobby in his spare time and on which he was well read. He worked first as a chemist with the Food and Drug Administration in Louisiana, pioneering a technique for sanitary shrimp production that is still used in the industry. During the Second World War, he served in the Pacific as a Japanese language specialist after studying at Yale University, ultimately working on General Douglas MacArthur's staff during the American occupation of Japan and contributing to policy decisions which influenced the future configuration and success of Japanese business and industry. In his last assignment, he moved to the Japanese island of Okinawa, where he worked for sixteen years in programs for the rehabilitation of the war-torn local economy.

The Oglesby Foundation was established to commemorate his work and benefit indigent students like himself who lack financial means to realize their goals for an education.

Sam Oglesby, the son of an island doctor, died on the island of Okinawa in December 1966 and was buried in the international cemetery there, halfway around the world from the island where he was born fifty-five years earlier. His mother, Nona Oglesby Bowen (in the 1930s, she remarried another waterman from the Eastern Shore named Clayton Jones Bowen), died shortly thereafter in Girdletree, in the house she and her family had lived in since they left Tangier. A grandson, Samuel Crockett Oglesby, Jr., recently retired from a career in the United Nations where, in the words of his grandmother, Nona Oglesby, he worked as a "globetrotter."

CHAPTER TEN
THE LAST EMPRESS

If She's Beautiful Enough,
Even a Gay Man Can Fall in Love

About a year ago, I got health-conscious and started cruising the city for juice bars. It wasn't an easy search. First of all, there aren't many of them around, and most of the ones I found were off-putting. There is the health food store variety – very expensive, with little plots of grass growing in the window that they turn into vile, thimble-sized shot glasses of bilious green liquid. The clientele are mostly yoga-types with pinched, pasty-pale faces who shoot you a side glance as if they know you still love bacon and margaritas. I just don't belong in those places and always get put down by the cashier when I ask a question, which ends up sounding stupid and causing more pursed lips and stares from the yoga victims. Then there are those spacey juice bars run by people who are really actors or play in a heavy metal band. I used to go to one on Columbus Avenue on the Upper West Side. The juicer had spiky hair and was always on his cell-phone, talking in an intimate, muffled way to somebody. No rapport with him. I need good vibes from my juice person. It's part of the holistic health experience. Besides being dirty and forgetting to peel off the apple labels, he kept unpredictable hours. People who are hooked need their juice fix on a regular schedule. I would rush there after my workout at the Y and they would be closed. It was too laidback and San Francisco for me. Then I found it. I mean her.

Just your basic Korean deli on the scruffy side of Third Avenue, at Forty-third Street. The usual tired fruit and spray-dyed daisies out front. I passed and heard the telltale whirring of a power juicer. Too late to stop because I had to make a train. Next day, I came back and my life changed. She stood behind the counter and smiled at me. Tall by any standard, especially for a Korean lady, with that cascading mountain of hair and her spiked heels, she was over six feet. Her coiffure was wonderful, kind of a mixture of Carmen Miranda and the Peruvian temples of Machu Picchu, climbing ever upwards, embellished by the smallest bouncy ringlets, which jiggled when she moved. And little bows and twinkly things tucked away here and there. Depending on the light, her hair was black or sometimes, if the sun was really bright outside, it shimmered with the slightest subtle touches of henna. Her skin was pale porcelain and there was little make-up except for the requisite eye accompaniments and your basic lipstick, which was always on the dark side. That gave her mouth a slightly dangerous look when she wasn't smiling. Kind of bee-stung lips that might belong to a sexy vampire. But when she smiled, her face lit up and two gorgeous big dimples appeared on either side of her mouth.

Her clothes were always just right. Sometimes black outfits that usually featured a tank top. This allowed exposure of her long, slender, firm arms and a full view of her swan-like neck. Then there was what I call her "denim and diamonds" look, close-fitting, pale blue levis and a jeans jacket studded with rhinestones and naughty little silver spikes. The way she moved behind the counter was wonderful. She could have been a supermodel on any big-time catwalk. Our first encounter was low-key and professional. I ordered my usual carrot, spinach and apple mix that she handed over to me with two hands in a slow, gliding motion. Very Asian and traditional. I thought of a tea ceremony I had witnessed some years ago. The most exquisite part was when she slowly peeled the paper off a straw and then, with a giggle, suddenly jabbed it into the cup cover. I got shivers. Throughout the operation, she always wore thin, translucent rubber gloves that she put on at the start and removed when finished. It was like she was a surgeon. I marveled how she took her time even when there were a lot of other customers.

Since I was dead serious about my juice routine, this meant nearly daily visits to the Last Empress. I gave her this name because there was really nothing else I

could call her. And did she fit the description or what!
Now, I never, ever called her that out loud or told her
about it. It was my secret. Maybe she had a secret name
for me too. Days passed and I became a regular. I didn't
even have to tell her what I wanted. She just saw me
coming, put on her gloves and did the job. Sometimes
we hardly spoke and, once in a while, I sensed she was
in a bad mood. That's when I would engage her in conversation. One day, I was humming while she juiced
and I mentioned that my hobby was cabaret singing.
She told me her hobby was golf, but that she was usually too busy to have a game. Things became more chal-
lenging a few days later when she said I could only have
my drink if I ordered in Spanish. Then she gave me
the three words I needed: *zanaoria* (carrot), *manzana*
(apple) and *spinaca* (spinach). She made me repeat
each of those words seven times so I wouldn't forget.
And I didn't. Even though she is gone now and I don't
need them any more.

I started to get a bit uneasy and confused about my
relationship with the Last Empress. I began to realize
that she was a flirt. Or let's say that most of the male
customers flirted with her and she gave it back to them.
That was normal and to be expected because she was
beautiful and had those dimples. If I didn't get with
the program and stop being nicey-nice and asking about
her golf game, I would probably just become history, as
far as she was concerned. But what could I do since I
had never flirted with a woman before? I had flirted
with lots of men and wasn't very good at it, so how could
I rise to the occasion with a lady, especially a busy one
where the window of opportunity for a flirt was, maxi-

mum, ten seconds? To strike it right in that amount of time, you had to be a well-practiced professional. I knew if I tried, I would be exposed as the gay impostor I was, trespassing on the other side's turf. I decided the way out was to lie. And I had to do it pretty quick because she had definitely drawn a line in the sand with me. As I left with my drink one day, she called out "*Hasta la vista*, baby!" Baby! She had never spoken to me like that before.

I knew this was it. She had upped the stakes in what, to me, was becoming a dizzy game. I developed my plan carefully. At the right time, it couldn't be forced or obvious, it just had to occur with perfect timing, I would casually say something like, "Last weekend, my wife and I went to the mall . . ." That would get me off the hook, so to speak. Free me from the flirting game without seeming like a cop-out wimp. Of course, I am not married, at least not to a woman. I do have a life companion or a domestic partner or whatever it is gay men living together call each other, but telling her the truth was obviously out of the question. So that was that. I would do it, and the sooner, the better.

The day arrived. It was now or never, and let's get it over with was all I could think about while I stood waiting for my juice. The Last Empress seemed so quiet. That gave me the opening I needed. But just as I started to speak, she handed me my *zanaoria, manzana, spinaca* and said with a smile, "Goodbye and thank you. This is the last time you're gonna see me." I took a very deep breath and tried not to cry. It was all so sudden. She told me she was moving to Forty-second and Eighth Avenue and was going to open her own small place. I said I would come there and be her regular customer, but I knew I would never see her again. I left quickly and went out on the street, looking back through the window at her, hoping to get in a final wave of the hand and a goodbye smile, maybe even a flirty one. But she was already talking and laughing with another customer. I was a little bit jealous.

The next week, I returned, wondering who would be her replacement. I dreaded what I would find. One time, months back, when she was on vacation, the deli owner made my juice. He was no fun and stingy and stinted on the ingredients. I didn't want to face him and get his less-than-full cup. What greeted me was an Asian version of Russell Crowe. He had very white teeth and lots of keys attached to his jeans, which were just as tight-fitting as the Last Empress's. His juices were even better than hers, if that were possible. After juicing, he added an extra special step. Instead of just pouring the juice into the cup and handing it to me, he'd transfer it to a blender and whip it up like a cappuccino. Wow!

So I guess things turned out okay, after all. I think about her sometimes and maybe I'll even go down to Forty-second Street for a juice one of these days. But not too soon. Otherwise, it will look like I'm in hot pursuit. Just a casual drop-in this summer, when it's hot and I need a drink. In the meantime, I'm very happy with the new arrangement and there's no problem with knowing how to flirt. If I ever have the chance.

CHAPTER ELEVEN
POSTCARD FROM UMBRIA

The Dark Side of Globalization

There is something about the breeze in Italy. It really does caress. Standing in the square by the Orvieto train station, the warm, bright sun forces me to squint. Through half-closed eyes – it's like looking through a filter which softens and blends the landscape – I gaze up at tall, gently swaying poplar trees and rich, earth-colored villas. The small piazza fountain dances in melodic splashes; the rhythm varies with a wind carrying that "Mediterranean" perfume – thyme and lavender – and an occasional whiff of strong coffee from the trackside café.

I am being met at the station for a week in the countryside near Todi, but for the moment, I couldn't care less about being picked up. Perhaps the transatlantic jet lag helps to give me that floating feeling; I want to do nothing but stand and be. The cicadas' buzz crescendos. I notice people, locals, some standing about, others sitting under the shaded canopy of a majestic chestnut tree, just doing sweet nothing. The Italians call it *dolce far niente*. They seem to have a word for all the good things in life.

My friend arrives on time. I wish he had been late. We toss my bags into the Fiat and begin our steep ascent up a winding road that curves through well-groomed fields of sunflowers and orchards of olive trees. The ancient hill town, Todi, glistens in the distance, its spires and towers strong against the blue sky. Majestically elevated and fortressed, it looks down in all directions like a maestro conducting a silent orchestra. Then I see them. I blink once, and then again, and I still see them. Standing by the road under the shade of a tree is a statuesque, young, black woman, clad in a miniskirt and a revealing halter. Her high heels push her well over six feet. She is beautiful. Is it Naomi Campbell on a fashion shoot in Italy? Has this young lady had a flat tire and is she waiting for the Italian AAA to come to her rescue? There is no car, but there is a bench behind her in the bushes. A hundred yards later, I see her sister, another tall, black woman; she waves and smiles. The lush, ancient Umbrian hills have become the backdrop for a new kind of business. The oldest profession in the world has become a multinational enterprise here in Todi. Master-minded and managed by the Albanian Mafia, operating out of nearby towns, centering on Perugia, these women, mostly African, are one department in a supermarket of vice and crime that has sprung up as part of the post-Cold War spread of globalization.

With the death of Enver Hoxha and the collapse of Euro-Communism's last holdout, Albanian crime made the short trip across the Adriatic to Italy, where it set up shop in drugs, prostitution, extortion and murder. This venture in globalization has been more than mildly successful; today, it is estimated that a large share of Middle Eastern and South Asian drugs are trafficked through these Albanian "businessmen," eventually finding their way to American markets. Today, Albanian-engineered crime is touching ordinary people, not just those with a penchant for dope and girls. As the crime machine expands and the rich grow richer, armed robbery has arrived in the peaceful, heretofore secure Umbrian countryside, where locks were more to keep livestock in than burglars out. A villa doesn't need to be unattended for more than a few hours. Trucks pull up, "clean house" and leave a spotlessly empty dwelling. Owners return and shock turns rapidly to relief. They're glad to be alive and know they can buy everything back at the well-known markets where stolen property is fenced. As with its homegrown counterpart, the Italian Mafia, highly publicized attempts at eradication are sporadic and largely ineffective, and the web of crime and vice grows quietly. Mafia experts are convinced that the organizations continue to thrive despite the thousands of arrests that have been made in recent years.

As we pull into the villa's driveway, I catch sight of the sparkling pool and talk turns to lunch and the afternoon's options for amusement. That night at dinner, I learn that Umbria has a new name: "Chianti-shire," so called for the legions of affluent English and Americans, together with the occasional Milanese day trader, who are buying up local property – any property – for astronomical prices. One wealthy expatriate recently flew in by helicopter to inspect a rather modest, rundown house that she purchased on the spot, saying it had "that wonderful quality of poverty about it." Other foreigners who bought early and cheap are cashing in with multi-million-dollar sales to the super rich. And what about ordinary local people – the *contadini?* They lack decent medical attention and the Italian pension program is broke. Where will they be in a few years? Burbling accounts of *bella* Tuscany and time-less Todi are charming, superficial and seemingly oblivious to the hard times, which are so easy to ignore in this beautiful, civilized land of smiles.

My week goes by in a flash. Mostly just sitting on the vine-covered verandah, looking happily out into the space before me – a valley climbing to gold-tinted, freshly plowed hills with purple mountains in the distance. A farmer's dog barks as the warm day fades and a cool evening brings out the big orange moon. The deep breaths of sweet air are delicious. People say just being in Umbria is a healing experience.

We start our descent to Orvieto, taking me back to

the train. The afternoon sun is hot and the sunflowers droop, waiting for relief from the cool night air. We pass the ladies on the road. They are tired too. They don't stand in fetching catwalk poses now. They sit, hunched over, looking at us with empty eyes as we pass and throw up dust in our wake. I wave to the tall beauty in heels. She fans herself with a newspaper and sends me a sad smile.

CHAPTER TWELVE
TOYOTA PICKUP, 1981, DRIVES LIKE NU

How a Liberated American Woman Joined a Polygamist's Harem Without Regret

I sat across the table from Makuna in a fly-infested teashop on the outskirts of Nairobi, looking down at the five-pound note. The fruit of our project to get rich. The wind blew up a spiral of dust that caused me to blink and my eyes teared up, more emotion than physical self-defense. What was I doing here, sitting in this forlorn Nowheresville, jet-lagged, hungry, being blamed by my husband for everything, from screwing up our business deal to not having his dinner ready on time? We had flown in from Japan for our honeymoon and a little transaction that would put money in our pockets. Makuna was Tokyo's hottest African musician. He played in the coolest Ginza clubs and had to fight off adoring *jimbos*, Japanese groupie-girls. But some-how, he liked me better, a redheaded Polish-American schoolteacher, looking forty in the face. Maybe it was my legs – I have great legs – or maybe because I loved to dance. I don't know why, but it worked. I had snagged one of the most desirable men in Tokyo and we were having the time of our lives. Now, in the middle of our honeymoon, everything was unraveling!

Since I left the States ten years earlier, my get-a-new-life plan had succeeded brilliantly: Find a good job and make money, have fun and forget the past. I had fled suburban Long Island and a dead-end mar-riage and Asia provided the change I needed: no-hassle teaching with respectful students and a social life that gave me my own space. Tokyo in the early '80s was an exciting place to be. My days were a blur of packed subway rides and back-to-back classes all over the city.

Nights I kept for myself, catching up on the good times my life had lacked for so many years. After a se-ries of short romances, I fell for Makuna, a six-foot-five-inch drummer from Zaire. Our time together was qual-ity and never dull. Lots of lovemaking, arguing and plan-ning the future of the band or just hanging out and being friends. One night in our second year together, I met Makuna after his club gig and we walked back to my place. He was uncharacteristically quiet. Suddenly he stopped, took my hand and said, "You are my wife." I accepted and found myself replying, "And you are my husband." When we got back to the flat, I asked him if he was really serious, and what about those other wives and kids in Africa? He told me they were "over there" and "my life is here with you." There was no church or courthouse, but from that moment, I had become his wife.

Between us, Makuna and I were pulling down big bucks, but having lots of money is never enough. We wanted more. The wheel of fortune seemed to spin our way one evening at dinner with Kenji-san, one of Makuna's backers in the club. He had made his fortune in used cars and said it was straightforward and very profitable. Now, Kenji-san wanted to tap the African market. We had been planning a trip to Africa, part honeymoon, part escape – Tokyo had its own kind of unbearable intensity – so why not turn this into a business trip too? Later that week, we booked a flight to Nairobi and bought a used pickup truck, financed by me. As our departure date approached, I grew excited. There were so many unknowns. By the time we boarded the plane for Nairobi, my stomach was in knots. Would I meet the other wives? Would they like me, this strange white woman who didn't speak their language? I prayed everything would work out. As the plane touched down, I became tense with anticipation.

At Kenyatta International Airport, the heat was oppressive as bodies jostled in the endless immigration queue, stale European odors mixing with the pungent smells of Africa. I almost forgot I had been here with my first husband nearly twenty years ago, when Kenya was all starched colonial linen and pith helmets. We had gone on a safari and I was called *Memsahib*. Now I was Makuna's wife, carrying his bag while he walked proudly ahead of me, waving to a clutch of family gathered by the taxi stand. As refugees, Makuna's clan lived on the poor fringes of Nairobi. After hours of snarling traffic in an ancient vehicle of mixed lineage, we entered the village in a cloud of red dust and lurched to a halt.

And there were the four wives. Tall and slender, old for their age, they stood barefoot in a row, silent and obedient. Makuna walked down the row, shaking their hands like a general reviewing his troops. I held back, waiting for the welcome of eye contact. We were shown to the best house in the compound, a cinderblock rectangle with metal roofing. As day faded, the one naked bulb in our room flickered its uncertain light onto the earth floor and I felt the whining touch of a mosquito.

After a sleepless night, I was aroused by the dawn call to prayer from a nearby mosque and the smell of wood smoke from breakfast fires. A woman appeared in the doorway with strong tea. While I sipped and rubbed my insect bites, she sat on the threshold, inspecting me with a tentative smile. I recognized her as one of the wives, probably the oldest one. No doubt my junior by a few years in spite of her wrinkles. She pointed to her face and repeated the word "Fatimah."

Makuna was nowhere in sight. I seemed to recall his leaving the hut in the middle of the night and I assumed he had sought the outdoor privy, but then I realized he was probably fulfilling long-overdue conjugal duties. Morning turned to afternoon, and I was alone. I had been dumped in this forlorn spot with my fellow wives while our master was at large somewhere.

Makuna arrived as the sun was setting and was in a bad mood. He told me the buyer had reneged on the original sale price for the pickup, saying it was not the right model Toyota. He now offered only a fraction of what we expected for my $8,000 investment. I protested that Kenji-san had specifically said Toyota pickup, but Makuna was beyond reason. I realized that he had been drinking and walked away to the hut. As I stood there swatting mosquitoes, Makuna approached, now in a rage, demanding his dinner. He grabbed me by the arm until it hurt, jerking me, doll-like, to him till our faces met. Why had I not prepared a meal for him? It was my duty as his wife! Anger battled confusion and I heard myself saying, "But where's the goddamn food to cook?" Makuna pointed to a scrawny chicken pecking its way across the earthen courtyard, slapped a machete in my hand and yelled, "*La voila!*" There it is!

Partly driven by fear, but mostly not knowing what to do except remove myself from his presence, I charged out into the courtyard, waving the knife. With the help of his other wives, we cornered the poor bird and Makuna's harem prepared his feast. I plucked while Fatimah boiled water, chopped cassava and poured cooking oil. We squatted around the fire while he ate loudly with belching satisfaction. One wife brought a finger bowl while another wiped his goatee. Stuffed and drowsy, our master nodded into a doze while we scrubbed the heavy cooking pots. I slept alone that night while Makuna made his rounds again. In a matter of hours, my honeymoon and the marriage it was supposed to celebrate were falling apart. Just as I now seemed to be disappointing him, Makuna had become a different man to me.

I awoke after a surprisingly good sleep. Stretching, I noticed a small blue mark on my soft inner arm where

Makuna had grabbed me. It still hurt. Fatimah was there with tea and a big smile. So were the other three wives. All five of us sat in silence for a few minutes. Their eyes traveled my body from head to foot and they exchanged giggles. Was I good at childbearing? How God-awful I must look, I thought. Then without knowing why, I began sketching on a tablet that lay on the table. I drew primitive stick figures of five women surrounding one very tall man. The wives burst into gales of laughter and hand clapping. One began a pantomime and pranced out to the courtyard. The others followed, pulling me to my feet. We danced and shouted till exhaustion forced us to the ground.

By the time Makuna had returned, my bags were packed. I told him I would see him in Tokyo, doubting that I would and caring less if we ever met again. He mumbled that we needed to talk and led me off to the village café. "You know, *ma cherie*, this first deal was just a trial run. The next time, we'll do it better. After all, what am I but an artiste, a drummer? These dirty business deals are not for creative people. I had to make so many 'noble gestures,' paying off this one, bribing that one. This government is a rat's nest. But trust your husband. And you can't say we ended up with nothing." I gazed at the five-pound note, worth about one dollar. The return on my $8,000 investment. Three months' hard work in the Tokyo rat race.

When we said goodbye, I went limp in Makuna's bear-like embrace, looking over his shoulder at the wives who watched us. As my plane climbed over Nairobi, I looked out at the red earth and dwindling rooftops below. My journey was almost over. Not the trip back to

Tokyo, but my return to reality. I thought of Fatimah and my other fellow wives. They would be with me wherever I went.

CHAPTER THIRTEEN
"24/7" – A PRISONER ON CENTRAL PARK SOUTH

After a Life of Adventure,
a Free Spirit Suddenly Finds Her Wings Clipped

Meg was always madcap, brilliant and different. In high school in the 1950s, she dyed her hair blue, played piano like Errol Garner without ever having a lesson, and had a pet mongoose named Riki Tiki Tavi. We were best friends. On summer afternoons, we'd hang out: lie on the grass and listen to the radio or go to her house and make music, me on the "drums" –

pounding on two old skillets – while she did her magic on the keyboard. Our favorite number was "Drum Negrita," an old George Shearing stand-by. Sometimes, Meg's dog, Queenie, would get in on the act and stand by the piano, howling. And we spent a lot of time just being silly. The silliest game we had was saying a word backwards. When our names became Mas and Gem, we rolled around, convulsed with laughter. Our parents always asked what made us laugh so hard.

After high school, we went our separate ways. College for both of us and then a stint in the Army for me. I saw her once when a bunch of us happened to be in Washington, D.C. for Christmas. Meg always specialized in making entrances and she certainly made one that winter day, when I met her flight at National Airport. She was coming from Miami and at first I didn't recognize her. I was looking for a college girl, but I found myself facing this femme fatale – frosted platinum hair, face Coppertone-brown with an inch of make-up, wearing a "pour-me-into-it" white knit dress and matching killer opera pumps, standing there like a B-movie Claire Trevor with an unlit Winston poised between her painted fingers. And a mountain of matching, powder-blue luggage for me to struggle with.

Years later – sometime in the '60s – I got a postcard from her. I was in Vietnam. The picture on the card showed a beautiful, old colonial-style hotel on one of the Hawaiian Islands. In the message on the back, she wrote that she was married and that she and her husband worked at that very hotel. She said they had been on their honeymoon there and that the hotel owner liked them so much, he asked them to stay and manage the place. Knowing Meg, that didn't surprise me. Amazing things like that just happened to her. I wrote to her, care of the hotel, but then we lost touch with each other.

This January, thirty-five years later, my kitchen phone rang. I picked it up and heard: "Mas, Gem here. Hey! I'm in New York City! High up over Manhattan, lookin' out at Central Park, and man, you know what I'm doin'? Ironing!" For the next hour, a monologue unfolded, filling me in on four decades of high life and adventure. The hotel gig in Hawaii lasted ten years and then got stale; too much drinking, fake friendliness and contrived hospitality. She escaped, going to sea with an Italian chef from Corsica, who had been on boats since he could walk. They sailed the world for twenty years in a forty-foot sloop, taking rich tourists to exotic islands like Sulawesi and Bali. One time, when the two of them were alone on the boat, they were becalmed for sixty days, just sailing in circles. They almost ran out of drinking water and the fish were too big to catch, but they survived. Meg said she read *War and Peace* three times and was never afraid, not one minute of the time. I believed her and somehow it all seemed normal. Amazing things always happened to Meg. Then her Italian chef died and she was getting old and there were bills to pay.

Which is what brought Meg to New York City and a new career at age sixty. She had joined the ranks of "household managers," becoming a live-in maid in a mega-bucks spread on Central Park South, working seven days a week. Her employer (we'll call her "Madame") is a Leona Helmsley-type: rich, once-beautiful and now, mostly a velvet-tongued nag. Total service without health insurance best described the job. Without regard to Meg's size or shape, Madame's first order was: "There are uniforms in the closet. Put one on." She is all things to Madame: cook, cleaning lady ("You missed some dust under the bed!"), and secretary ("Never LICK an envelope. It JUST isn't done! We must SEAL them with a damp sponge!").

But that's not all. Meg is also Madame's friend. Madame has few friends and often dines alone. But not anymore. Meg is there. Sometimes, Meg gets a few hours off if Madame goes to the opera or a benefit. But there is never total freedom. Even on time off, Meg must tell Madame where she is going and leave a phone number. Just in case. Life has its trade-offs, Meg tells me stoically. What's to complain about when you live and eat on Central Park South and get $3,500-a-month salary? And I say to her, "What's to complain about is: You're not even getting the minimum wage. When you divide "24/7" into three-and-a-half grand, that works out to less than five bucks an hour! Do the math!"

But who am I to tell her what to do? Now, when Meg calls me, most of her chat consists of anecdotes about Madame. She tries to make them sound funny, and I know she is trying hard to make a virtue of necessity. I usually end up feeling sad or mad when I listen to her stories. I think of a free spirit who's had her wings clipped. Trapped in a gilded cage and all that.

Meg tells me it's a breeze working for a man compared to having a female employer. Before she started working for Madame, Meg was employed by an elderly gentleman, who was kind and not very demanding. That job didn't last long. She had to leave when he had a stroke, since lifting him was more than she could handle. So there she is with Madame. Meg reports that there is a bit of light at the end of the tunnel. Madame smiled for the first time the other day.

I'm planning a big party at my house this summer, mainly to celebrate being eligible for social security. Lots of friends are invited and we're having a live rock-and-roll band called Kruize Kontrol. I met the band in the Fifty-first Street subway, where they play for rush-hour crowds. They are great and very loud. Meg said she would come to the party if she can get away. I hope she comes. And I hope Madame calls her here while we are swinging to the sweet sounds of the band. I'll make sure the sound system is really turned up. Maybe it will have a magic effect on Madame. But I doubt it. She'll probably just say something like, "Meg, what's all that racket? And by the way, have you been dipping into my Chanel Number 5? There isn't much left and I haven't used it since Charlie died."

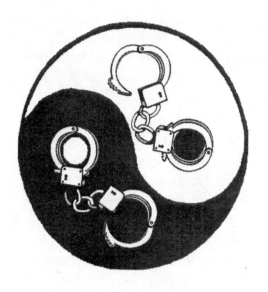

CHAPTER FOURTEEN
CPR AND THE NYPD

Take away dignity and you have hate. We despise those who strip us of this essential human quality and loathe ourselves in the bargain. The resulting debasement exemplifies our criminal justice system's failure to deal intelligently with petty crimes and misdemeanors so these "gateway" activities won't happen again or escalate to more serious criminal behavior. The police department's insensitive, heavy-handed – some would say cruel – treatment of first-time offenders not only misses the golden opportunity to set people on the right track and gain their respect, creating more law-and-order advocates; it also unnecessarily alienates the targets of its arrests, often driving them down the path of no return to repeated offenses. For CPR – courtesy, professionalism and respect – to be more than a cop car logo, changes must be made at the NYPD.

My own recent experience is a small window on a system gone wrong. I am a middle-aged professional with a squeaky-clean record ("Ever arrested? Are you kidding?"). Well educated, homeowner and all that. Support law and order? You bet. Well, maybe with a few reservations after my bout with the law. It went like this:

12:30 P.M. – A bright Indian summer day in November. I was apprehended for hopping a subway turnstile. Flash of a badge and a viselike grip on my arm as I was led away. Attempts to talk were silenced by threats of getting rough. Became frightened and confused. Handcuffed and taken to a police station. Photographed, paperwork.

1:30 P.M. – Locked in a cell. Belongings, including eyeglasses taken away ("Ya don't need 'em, ya not gonna read nothin'"). Asked how long I would be held, said I had to go to work. No reply.

2:30 P.M. – Taken to another police station, put in another cell. Wanted a drink of water, needed to use the toilet. Nobody heard my requests.

4:00 P.M. – Fingerprinted and moved to another cell. Finally led, hands behind back, to an open-door toilet. Cop watched while I relieved myself.

5:30 P.M. – Getting hungry, hadn't eaten since breakfast. Told we were going "downtown", transferred to a small holding cell. Cellmate a wild-eyed "pro," nonstop

talker: lurid accounts of police brutality, inmate violence. Fear of the uncertain was competing with the boredom of waiting. Hadn't waited so much since Army days.

7:30 P.M. – Hands and face against the wall, fleeced
and handcuffed chain gang-style to five other prisoners.
Experienced an irrational rush of euphoria – at least we
were moving and I was getting away from my cellmate. I
had nicknamed him "Willard."

8:30 P.M. – Loaded into a windowless paddy wagon with
no ventilation. Pitch dark. Side benches seated a total of
twelve; there were twenty-four of us. Old guy who limped
had to stand. Web of chains prevented offering him a seat.
Fear and lack of air made breathing difficult. Could it possibly get worse? Yes! Cigarettes lit and passed around. Almost partook in a desperate attempt at camaraderie and
diversion. Felt I was "losing it." Handcuffs tight around my
wrists. Hands losing circulation, arthritic joints throbbing
with pain. Wanted to scream. Then slipped into a limp
state born of resignation, a sense of defeat and a shred of
thankfulness that, at least, I had a seat. Paddy wagon bumping and swaying. Somebody said we were headed down
the West Side Highway. Old guy wearing a Korean War Vet
baseball cap started yelling, wanted to sit down, hated white
people. Somehow, with a shuffle of chains, we changed
places. Quiet now except for policewoman in the cab talking about her boyfriend's motorcycle. Suddenly I smell burning wool. Somebody's jacket is on fire from a cigarette.
Remember my grandmother telling me, "Everything in
life has meaning and a reason, and happens for the best."

9:30 P.M. – Slivers of neon through the slit in the cab.
We stop and an old timer says we have arrived at Center
Street. Thank God! At least we can get out and move and

breathe. How sweet simple things are! Walking unfettered, fresh air! Even the subway seemed like a national park! Not so fast! Told we're not going anywhere yet. The Riker's Island buses have offload priority. It's like that in life: The toughest always go first. We all start screaming. Some good, full, deep voices. Some whiny howls. I almost cry and laugh at the same time, realizing I had a grand-tier seat at the Met that night for Carmen. I'm really starting to lose it.

10:00 P.M. – We stumble out of the wagon into the cold night air. From here on it's an increasing blur: Bright, bright lights. The paddy wagon was hot and dark; Center Street is cold and glaring. You can't have everything. I'm beyond hunger and wanting to urinate. Maybe this is what nirvana is like. I seem liberated from physical needs. More paperwork and photographs. This time front AND profile shots. And lift your chin high for the camera! I felt like those elite, prancing Soviet honor guards at Lenin's Tomb with their arrogant, upraised faces. I start to cry, thinking of the last time I heard my mother's voice eighteen years ago over a crackly international connection when she called me overseas from the hospital, gasping to say goodbye. Why are we still chained up? Obviously, nobody's going anywhere!

11:00 P.M. – We "check in" for the night. Our cell can hold twenty. There are thirty-five of us. A dinner of baloney sandwiches is served, but there are only four sandwiches. It must be near freezing outside, but the jail cell is air-conditioned. One guy is wearing only a T-shirt. I'm lucky. For some reason, I put on long johns that morning. No place on the metal wall bench to sit. Can't sit on the floor because it's filthy and freezing. Open toilet stinks.

2:00 A.M. – After standing for a couple of hours, maybe more, I try to squeeze on the bench next to a big guy who is reclining, using up five seating spaces. He hits me and shoves me on the floor. I stay there.

4:00 A.M. – Breakfast is served. Cornflakes in a box and milk. My neighbor spills his on me and I give mine to another guy. Two well-dressed inmates grip the cell bars and taunt the police; the cops hurl insults back. Our prisoner population is constantly changing as courtroom calls deplete and refill the cell.

8:00 A.M. – I'm transferred to a cell upstairs and interview with a Legal Aid Society lawyer. He tells me I have committed a "violation," which is less than a misdemeanor, and recommends I accept a day's community service and get it all behind me. Otherwise, trials mean time and money. I still don't think I committed any offense. He also tells me the police could have issued a summons and that the whole night in jail was unnecessary.

11:00 A.M. – I stand before the judge and accept a day's community service. The sound of her gavel is still in my ears as I savor the freedom and sunlight on the street.

Was it all necessary? I'm still seeking out Granny's truism about things happening for the best. While I ponder, I can't help but feel it was a waste of everybody's time and money. And I'm still struggling with post-arrest syndrome: loathing, confusion and mostly, fear of cops. I guess I'll get over it. I have to.

CHAPTER FIFTEEN
POSTCARD FROM NANTUCKET

Notes from a Labor Day Lemming

Around midnight, the SUV herds disappear and Main Street Nantucket is quiet. A few stragglers – well-heeled diners in blazers and Ann Taylor outfits – wander to the end of the dock and step down into the luxury of their bobbing pleasure craft. Flickering street lamps set shadows dancing on the brick sidewalks and cobblestones glisten under a light mist. A tongue of fog creeps up from Straight Wharf. As the clock ticks, decades slip away. Nantucket is still a whaling town. I walk the empty streets, amazed at how pristine it all still is. Every summer, between Memorial and Labor Day, the island's population explodes from 9,000 natives to nearly 100,000 "off-islanders," pleasure-seekers drawn to this bastion of WASP culture. But even with the crowds and T-shirt shops that sell baseball caps for twenty-two dollars, Nantucket is a good place to be.

This three-day jaunt from New York City has cost me plenty. Double what a trip to Europe would be. It's the price I pay for caving in to impulse and booking two days before Labor Day. Always wanted to visit Nantucket, so here I am. Through the rain, we steal in from the airport on Friday night and the taxi drops us in front of the clapboard guesthouse on Fair Street. We spend a good part of the following day at the Whaling Museum, spellbound by the lore that unfolds in what must be one of the more compelling stories in American history. How a tiny, windswept island became one of the richest towns in America, so famous that it figured in a speech before the British Parliament in 1775. The epic quality of whaling in its heyday is hard to surpass in terms of heroics, danger and sheer adventure, not to mention the incredible riches it brought to the Quakers who exploited these majestic animals whose brains alone weighed a ton or more.

Then the bubble broke and it was all over suddenly when oil was discovered in a Pennsylvania field in 1869. But their houses still stand. Not the grand palaces that Venice built with its riches, just stolid salt boxes clothed in weathered gray shingles. Saturday night, we go to the movies. The best part is the old-fashioned, small-town cinema house itself. Tickets are those tiny, crudely printed sections off a roll which I hadn't seen since the 1950s and the audience are mostly locals, easy to spot by their dress and the way they look – people who have that "island" look, lots of prominent noses and receding chins, the same result of generations of in-breeding you see in other isolated places in West Virginia and the Chesapeake Bay.

Dining in Nantucket is a WASP experience. In spite of the wealth and apparent sophistication – albeit of a Bush Republican variety – of the well-heeled lemmings who pack the restaurants, forming queues as late as 11:00 P.M. to get into the "hot" places, the food is incredibly boring. Good, mind you, but boring. All very uniform. Elegant surf and turf, if that is possible. Not one Thai or Vietnamese or Korean place to be found. By Night Three, our New York City taste buds were raging against the lack of diversity. We finally find a spot on the edge of town with the name "Wok" in it and have our spicy rice dish fix.

The only hint at diversity is the flood of Bulgarians in Nantucket. Bulgarians? They are everywhere. Twenty-somethings who work in service jobs, mostly cashiers and waiters, they move about robot-like with virtually no knowledge of English. After several unsuccessful attempts at basic communication, I finally realize the young woman selling me a T-shirt was only equipped linguistically to repeat the numbers on the cash register. Later, I ask a waitress (from Iowa) where they all came from. She shrugs and says, "The word got out and they just appeared," whatever that meant.

Saturday, I go to Evensong at the local Episcopal Church. A beautiful gingerbread affair with the most amazing stained-glass windows. An aging pastor leads the service in a quavering voice. The old guard is still there, but for how much longer? My own Nantucket adventures were rather tame – being locked inside the local pharmacy and having to escape through the cellar's back door when the manager couldn't find his key, and creating a traffic jam as I wobbled up the Cliff Road bike path, trying to find third gear as other cyclists shouted "Passing on the left!" at me. I'll go back to Nantucket again. Maybe by then, the Bulgarians will speak some English and the SUV drivers will have switched to bikes. Whatever happens, the whalers will be there, their ghosts reaching out from behind shingled houses as midnight approaches and the fog rolls in.

Artwork and design by Aimal Arbab, Freddie Maung Oo and Dede Supriati. Photos from the files of the author, Aimal Arbab, Freddie Maung Oo and William Johnson.

GBP